T0065789

ANGELIC WITNESS TO THE KING OF GLORY

RALPH EBOTMANYINAW

WESTBOW
PRESS®
A DIVISION OF THOMAS NELSON
& ZONDERVAN

WestBow Press books may be ordered through booksellers or by contacting:

WestBow Press
A Division of Thomas Nelson & Zondervan
1663 Liberty Drive
Bloomington, IN 47403
www.westbowpress.com
844-714-3454

Scripture quotations taken from The Holy Bible, New International Version® NIV® Copyright © 1973 1978 1984 2011 by Biblica, Inc. TM. Used by permission. All rights reserved worldwide.

Scripture taken from the King James Version of the Bible.

ISBN: 978-1-6642-6684-1 (sc)
ISBN: 978-1-6642-6686-5 (hc)
ISBN: 978-1-6642-6685-8 (e)

Library of Congress Control Number: 2022909139

Print information available on the last page.

WestBow Press rev. date: 06/28/2022

CONTENTS

Angelic Witness to The King Of Glory

ANGELIC WITNESS TO THE KING OF GLORY presents a discussion of the role that angels of God played in the Incarnation of our Lord Jesus Christ. The book also discusses what I call the seven titles of deity given to the Baby-Lord. The term Angelic Witness is the same thing as angels testifying or witnessing about the King of Glory. The testimony about the Lord Jesus came from what angel Gabriel gave us when he appeared to Mary, the mother of our Lord in which he described who the Lord was and would be.

The Incarnation is one of the most hotly debated issues in human history, especially among the Jews. As the story goes most of the people of Israel denied that He even came, because He did not meet their requirements of their Messiah. This book refutes Jewish claims, and documents testimonies about His birth, early life, death, burial and resurrection. I believe that that record is stored up in the archives of God in heaven forever. The evidence includes those of us whom He has saved and continues to save all over the world.

One of our goals is to prove that Jesus Christ is the same Living God of the universe. The divinity of Christ is only a small part of the book, the greater part is about angels: who they are, and what they do. In discussing the subject of angels, we have attempted to bring clarity to the confusion that surrounds these supernatural beings.

Angel Gabriel had been with the Master for ages, so he knew Him intimately as his Lord. In fact, he had just left Him moments before he came to earth that day. Every word, title or description he gave points to the fact that Jesus Christ is God just as God the Father, and the Holy

Spirit. Gabriel traced His deity from the past to when He will physically assume His throne on this earth during the Millennial Reign.

In chapter 1, the book discusses the King of Glory, with emphasis on the deity of *the child*. It explains Five of the Seven Titles given by the angel namely: Jesus, Son of the Highest, King of Kings, Everlasting King, and Holy Son of God. Secondly, we look at Mary's Faith as a requirement of any calling, when it comes to accepting to bear the Great Child or not.

Chapter 2: The King of Glory, centers on the Birth of the King, and continues with the theme of Deity, speaking discussing how the TRIUM God functions and explaining the rest of the Two Titles namely: Christ and Lord. The rest of the Chapter discusses in-depth His earthly life: Who Christ is; the Son of Man and Son of God. Other issues concerning the Lord's humanity, Christ as the Indwelling Spirit, and other issues of deity: His Omniscience, All Wise God, power to create, power to sustain, and Prince of Peace. Chapters 3, 5, 6, 7 and 8 are devoted to angels as His servants.

While most of the Book is about Holy angels, Chapter 4 is about Evil angels and the fall of Satan. A provocative question has been raised and answered: Could Satan create his own universe? In this must-read chapter, the author brings out the folly of Satan in the communication between God and the devil, his misunderstanding of his environment, his ignorance concerning God, and his total suicidal mission of engaging in a war, he knows he can never win.

Chapter 9 discusses the Angelic Witness of The Lord's Glorious Resurrection. In view of the lack of knowledge surrounding angels the book presents a biblical and only view of angels. Chapter 10 focuses on the beginning of the Church of Jesus Christ and the important part of Angelic Involvement in the events that unfold in the process of establishing the church. Emphasis is placed on what constitutes a Church, and the importance of the Holy Spirit and His power in the Church. Chapter 11 speaks of LESSONS learned about angels, and chapter 12 brings the Book to its Conclusion.

CHAPTER 1

The King is Coming

The King is coming is about the news of the King of Glory, Jesus Christ, who took human form and came to this earth. His momentous advent according to biblical accounts, witnessed the invasion of heavenly hosts upon Bethlehem for a celebration that defies description. It was the first time that heaven and earth came together, the joy of which still looms over the earth till today. Christmas, the day of His birth still reminds us year after year of that first glorious morning. Nothing parallels it the world over.

As great as Christmas is, not much is clear about the details of who this Mighty Personality is, judging from the differing views of the church. This has given room to fables, and all kinds of stories surrounding Christmas, reducing it to a mere holiday. Some denominations believe that He was fully God, others believe that He was fully man. Some say He was both God and man. Yet others still say that He was nothing more than a good man, and a great Teacher. The question that we must address is how can One so great and mighty vanish from the memories of those He came and died to save?

The challenge of Angelic Witness is to dispel the myths surrounding Jesus Christ and to bring clarity to the nature of this Most Glorious Personality that ever hit the earth. From the lips of His own angels, as recorded in the pages of the Holy Bible, Angelic Witness brings forth the undisputed truth about this Incarnate Deity.

In Bible times angels were basically part of Israelite society. They made frequent visits to sites there. We know that an angel came to the pool of Bethsaida, (John 5:1-5) at appointed times in the year to stir up the pool to bring healing to some people who had chronic diseases. In those times people who had these issues would show up at the pool, but only those who were able to get into the pool when it was stirred, would receive their miracle.

One very special day the angel of the Lord was sent by God not to the pool, this time, but to a young virgin called Mary, engaged to be married to a young man, named Joseph, with a very different type of message. When the angel came to Mary he said to her:

"Fear not Mary, for you have found favor with God and behold you will conceive in your womb, and bring a son, and you shall call His name JESUS. He shall be great and shall be called the Son of the Highest: and the LORD God shall give Him the throne of His father David; and He will reign over the House of Jacob forever, and of His kingdom there shall be no end." Mary said to the angel, "how shall this be, seeing I know not a man?" The angel said to her, "the Holy Ghost shall come upon thee, and the power of the Highest shall overshadow thee, and therefore, this Holy Thing which shall be born of thee shall be called the Son of God." (Luke 1:27-35)

From the passage I sense that the words of the angel were exciting, almost musical. News of a new baby is already wonderful, but Mary was caught up in the wonder of it that she didn't quite understand the grandeur of the angelic report. As we know now the One to be born was no ordinary Child, so we have to get into Gabriel's head to help us understand who this extraordinary Personality really is. From the passage above we picked up seven divine titles that were given to the Baby including: **Jesus, Son of the Highest, Ruler, Eternal God,** the **King of Kings, Christ,** and **Lord.** In the sections following we shall discuss five of these titles, and the last two will be discussed in the next chapter. In that way we shall see how anyone can be mistaken about this Personality being anything other than God.

When angel Gabriel came to Mary his message was, "you have found favor with God," and behold you will conceive in your womb and bring forth a son." What a message, and what does "finding favor with God" mean? In today's language the phrase found favor means:

you are blessed by God. You see Mary was not used to any of these considering her low estate or status from the backwoods of Nazareth. All this sounded like a dream, especially when it was connected to the Almighty God. She might have been thinking: "who are you and what are you talking about? Do you even know me?" That's why she was troubled by the angel's statements, but Gabriel just persisted.

The word Behold stands out here too, and it calls attention to the reality of what is going to happen, something big, or something great. It seemed as if, the angel was watching the event happen in heaven. Behold says, 'look or wow, and often associated with the fact that something big is taking place. In this case it is speaking of the great Personality that was to be born.

Throughout the delivery the angel was excited. News about childbirth is always exciting, especially this One. He continued with the same attitude, especially when he found out that Mary's cousin, Elizabeth was already pregnant. The whole situation just became so exciting. We can make that assumption, because Mary exploded with excitement of her own as she accepted the report of the angel: **"Be it unto me according to thy word."** (Luke 1:38)

JESUS

The angel said, "You shall call His name Jesus." (Luke 1.31) The name **Jesus** is a Hebrew name for God which is to say Savior. The name gives us the reason for His coming, which is. "to save His people from their sins." (Matthew 1:21) That means He is the sin-bearer, and the only one at that. The name is used a lot in the Book of Isaiah, the Messianic Book especially chapter forty-three for God Himself who assured His people that He would save them even from the fire.

This chapter means a lot to me. It was from here that I received my own salvation based on these verses: Isaiah 43:18-19 The Lord reminded me that I still had a life after my father passed away. For a while I saw no purpose of continuing to live, and I fell into a depression that took several years to heal. The word of God stated: "Remember not the former things, I will do a new thing; shall it not come forth?" After reading that I realized that the devil had been feeding me a steady diet of my past, and he got me thinking that I could not live after my father passed. I held on to the thoughts about my late father, and the more I did the deeper I sank into the depression. As I studied the text, those verses grabbed my attention. I knew that I should look to God instead. With this new knowledge I was immediately healed from the disease.

I have never saved anyone, and neither have you. From what the bible teaches us we know that it takes the blood of Jesus, and its power to take away or bear the sins of mankind. We know that sin causes pain, and death. Imagine the sins of the whole world. Jesus took the sins of all mankind in His own body. We can only imagine what an impossible task that could have been, but then that's why He is not an ordinary Man. He is the Savior of the world.

He is the only Person who can redeem us. Nobody could do it. Angels couldn't. From what we know now the Savior must be a Super, Super Natural Being. As He took human form, scripture says He retained His divine nature. That's why He was tempted and tried, but He never failed. (Matthew 4:4) This redemption exercise was so great that it took the Son of God to do it. Only His blood and power can save. If you use my blood it will not help anyone. Another name associated with Him is the Lamb of God. He is the very God Himself.

As I stated above the savior had to be a Super Natural Human to save mankind. Only God in human form can perform this task. He had to come in the flesh, possessing the pure blood of God. That's why His coming was very important, and critical, and it's like a-do-or-die situation, for without Him the whole human race would have been lost. The Savior is therefore undeniably God.

THE SON OF THE HIGHEST

Gabriel also said, "He will be great, and He shall be called the Son of the Highest." (Luke 1:32) The term Son of God has confused the world for ages. Let us see what Scripture says about it. The Son of God is not a person gotten through human procreation. The bible says He was obtained by divine decree, because He has always existed with the

Father. (Psalm 2:7) According to this Psalm God the Father simply declared part of Himself Son, saying, "this day have I begotten thee." He is part of God that was destined to become human.

The name Highest is identified with the Almighty God of the Highest heaven. That is the part of heaven inhabited only by the divine in the exclusive realms of glory. According to the Book of Ezekiel, this is the highest heaven. As He saves us this is where we are seated with Him. Some think that makes us higher than all other beings. That's true, but don't forget, we did not earn it. It is through Him. So, the Son of God is the Son of the Highest Heaven.

KING OF KINGS

The next thing the angel said was "the Lord God shall give Him the throne of His father David." He will therefore be a king, taken from among prior kings of Israel. Other translations say, "He shall **sit** on the throne of His father David." The word sit speaks of permanence. David was the best king of Israel, and therefore Christ will rule over his kingdom, because he was an earthly and temporary king who will die. That means this King will be the King of all Kings. David was given the kingdom on a temporary basis until the rightful King came. Listen to what God said to David: "when thy days shall be fulfilled, thou shalt sleep (die) with thy fathers. I will set up thy Seed (JESUS) after thee, which will proceed out of thy bowels; I will establish His kingdom. He shall build a house for My Name, and I will establish the throne of His Kingdom forever." Therefore, Jesus is King of all kings. (2 Samuel 7:12-16)

THE ETERNAL

The angel proceeded: "He will reign over the house of Jacob forever. And of His kingdom there will be no end." He takes over the kingdom and rules forever, making Him the Eternal God." (Luke 1:33) No other king could rule forever except Christ. So, He is the Eternal God. Jesus was above death, and that's what was on God's mind.

The question is, how can anyone confuse Who He is? It was spelt out right from the beginning before His birth. He was to sit in the throne of His father David. As King, He was the eternal Ruler.

HOLY SON OF GOD

This was strange news, and it was difficult to grasp. Mary wondered, "how can this be, seeing I have never known a man?" Gabriel explained calmly in verse 35, "the Holy Ghost shall come upon you, and the power of the Highest shall overshadow you, therefore, this **HOLY THING** that shall be born of thee shall be called the Son of God." There was no mention of Mary and Joseph as being born holy. There are denominations that include Mary, and Joseph and even His other siblings in the description of His holiness. The only thing that was to be born of Mary was the Lord. Therefore, there is no scriptural basis for some type of holy family that was to be born. A holy family was never born anywhere in the world. Jesus is the only Holy Son of God.

The word holy or holiness is a special word. Holiness sets God apart, because it is His Character. To set Him apart means He is the only one who is holy. Sometimes, He tends to share this quality with those around Him. That's why the Lord Jesus calls His angels holy. Otherwise, no one else is holy.

Holy means that God is undefiled, pure and perfect. He is so pure His face radiates light. That's why angels cover their faces. I had a dream one of the few times and I saw the Lord, but I could not see His face. In this dream I was brought to the day of His crucifixion. As the Roman soldiers were whipping Him He fell down under the cross. I thought, "This was my time to help." I jumped in with a machete to cut the chains. Then the Lord turned and looked at me as if to say, "What are you doing my friend?" As He did He looked at me very sternly and His eyes were like this blazing light, like the sun at the height of its power. The light from His eyes blinded me and I fell off. So, I could not see His face. At least I know without a doubt that I saw Him on the way to the crucifixion.

God is the only One who is Holy, because He is pure, perfect, and sovereign. He is above all things, and He alone sets the rules upon which the universe operates. He is the only One who can stand outside the universe.

MARY'S FAITH

I am sure it all came to Mary's faith. Did she have the faith to go along with this divine calling? The answer to this question may have many parts. In the first place it was a calling of God just like any other. No one knew the basis of God's choices, but we know He never makes mistakes, and whatever He does is always right and perfect. Throughout the ages many people have been chosen by God the same way. She, like others, was called to fulfill this tremendous duty. We know that she did not apply to be chosen. True, no one does. We also know that by His infinite wisdom things like these always go according to His will. Only God knew the answers, and we know that she was God's perfect Choice, because He knew that Mary would have the faith she needed.

It turned out she said yes. She did this ignoring the shame and disgrace. It sounded surprising for someone who was engaged to be married to another man. Mary was a great woman of faith. Interestingly, the Son she bore was to go through the same thing His mother went through in terms of suffering.

GOD'S POWER

The greatest credit goes to the Lord Himself. Mary could have refused to avoid the confusion, and disgrace that would follow, but this is another proof of His omniscience. A lesson for us to learn is that when God speaks we cannot look for further evidence. That's why Gabriel came. What Mary did is not less than what Abraham did. She had the backing of God, and that was all there was to it.

THE ACCEPTANCE

After the meeting with the angel, acceptance rumors were swelling, accusers were increasing, and pressure was mounting. Finger-pointing was all around her. Did she have the faith to help her make this great decision? Usually it's one thing to say yes, dealing with the problems that follow is another thing.

The call of God sometimes comes with problems and complications. For example, it does not make sense for a woman who is engaged to be married to another man to accept bearing a child from another. God knew that. Her fiancé was also threatening to put her away privately. That was because he was ashamed of what had happened to Mary. Don't forget that the devil was in on this too. He was giving her his own ideas. It all came down to Mary and God. That was in Mary's mind too. She struggled alone with the decision. All people do. Finally, the answer came: "be it unto me according to thy word." (Luke 1:38)

The calling of God comes with risks. Mary had become a national disgrace, and the local newspapers had no mercy. They had it blasting at full throttle. All eyes were on her. This is when people who know you very well abandon you. A private girl, one who was trusted by everyone became one nobody could trust. She had become the target for publicity. For one moment there she was a symbol of purity, but that day she became the object of all kinds of negativity.

The Lord was with her, and her answer never changed. She knew what she was going through, yet the answer remained what we know today, as the greatest acts of faith ever known. We owe our salvation to that answer. In a way she, like her Son after her who paid the ultimate prize, and indeed: "all people throughout the world shall call her blessed." (Luke 1:48) Amen.

CHAPTER 2

The King of Glory

ANGELS WITNESS HIS BIRTH

The King of Glory is the King of Heaven, and that is our Lord, Jesus Christ. One of the missions of Christ was to make God known to the people of Israel and the world. Scripture reveals One God in Three Persons: The Father, the Son, and the Holy Spirit. (John 14:6-17). These Persons are equal in being and in Essence.

According to Benny HINN, author of Good Morning Holy Spirit, he likened God to the process of these three Persons creating a light bulb where God the Father is the **Idealist**, the one who introduces the idea of creating a light bulb. He might say: let us make the light. Since the Holy Spirit is in the Father and the Son, that idea of creating a light is communicated automatically to the Son by the Spirit. The Son then **designs** or **creates** the light bulb. That's why the Son is in fact the Creator of all things. The idea is already known by the Holy Spirit, who then gives the electric Power, and that completes the creation of the light bulb.

Remember we called the Father the idealist, or Commander, the Son, the Creator, or Designer, and the Holy Spirit, the Power of God. These are just titles to help explain what the Godhead probably does. These may not be what they do. The main reason for all this is to try to explain why Jesus Christ is the Creator of all things. The truth is no one truly knows how these three Persons operate.

With that understanding the universe was created. The King of

Glory is the King of Heaven and He is the actual Creator of all things as we saw above. The Lord Jesus Christ Created all things visible and invisible including angelic Beings. Spirit beings of any kind were all created by our great Maker. That is why the angels took part in His Incarnation. He is their King also. Just as the military and other members of the defense department accompany the president of the U.S. on trips anywhere angels did the same thing as the Lord of Glory came to earth.

The question is what type of angels came? It was not surprising to note what the bible said: "suddenly a great company of heavenly or angelic hosts appeared with the angel." Luke 2:13) The hosts are the Lord's military. They appeared in Bethlehem praising God. How many were they? It says a great number, maybe millions. When you combine the number and the glory of God that filled the air that day, the scene defied description. That was a glorious, glorious event. Scripture shows us that they were with Him the whole time He was on earth. We will be discussing angelic hosts in chapter 7.

A question came up at His trial by the Sanhedrin saying: "are you a king? He answered: "My kingdom is not of this world, if my kingdom were of this world then would my servants fight." (John 18:35-37) Those servants are His angelic hosts who have unlimited strength. He confirmed the answer to our question in the very next verse: "You say that I am a King. To this end was I born, and for this cause came I into this world." So, when He used words like My, or His, that was not just talk. He created them, and He owns them. He has also used similar terms for His angels: reapers, gatherers and servants, etc. (Matthew 13:28-39) During that time they were prepared, and waited for His call, but it never came. That was not their job. They showed up on various occasions when He took time to pray and they made other appearances to minister to Him. All along they were there, and they learned everything that He taught the apostles.

THE RESPONSE

"Behold the handmaid of the Lord," Mary responded to what the angel said, and the power of God overcame her, and she was conceived. Her words were some of the most powerful statements of faith ever made, because they were full of faith, risky, and fully trusting. Here is a woman who was engaged to be married to another, yet she agreed to carry the child in her womb given by another. (Luke 1:38)

That was a great answer. It sounded like the kind of response that you receive when you minister to someone about receiving Christ. You think this person is not going to answer in affirmative, but before you know it, you hear: "yes I will accept the Lord." Her answer was what God expected. It was like a home run.

In Jewish circles people probably had different thoughts: "has she lost her mind? How can a person engaged to another man accept to bear a child from another? What about Joseph? That poor man, what is he going to do?" We know that these were small villages and communities, word went around very quickly. The news was all over town the next day. It was the talk at breakfast, lunch, and dinner. Mary made the headlines of the local newspapers and the Jerusalem TV News that day, next day, and several days following, but who cares?

She was ridiculed all over town. I know that because Joseph wanted to put her away privately. She was viewed in all kinds of ways and no one would associate with her. No one had ever heard of such a thing. The innocent and most favored young girl in the city suddenly became an outcast, even by her own fiancée. Put yourself in her place and see how you cope.

Sometimes it takes a scandal like this to up. No, he will stick it to you. Sometimes you are caught between the word of God and your faith. This is where the virgin mother found herself. You would think a country girl like this would be weeping all over the place, but surprisingly Mary defied all that name-calling and went for the slam dunk or believed. Scripture does not say whether she got mad about it or picked fights with anyone. Then help came, as the angel of the Lord appeared to Joseph, who was battling with his own faith saying:

> "Joseph, son of David, do not be afraid to take Mary as
> Your wife, for the child who has been conceived in her
> is of the Holy Spirit. She will bring forth a Son, and you
> Shall Call His name Jesus, because He will save His
> people from their sins." (Matthew. 1:20-21)

That answer to the doubting mind of Joseph came too late after Mary had made up her own mind about what the angel told her. What a brave young woman!

THE MAGNIFICAT

GREATEST WORDS OF FAITH: "Behold the handmaid of the Lord, be it done unto me according to their word. My soul doth magnify the Lord, and my spirit has rejoiced in God, my Savior. For He hath regarded the low estate of His handmaid: for, behold, from henceforth all generations shall call me blessed. For He that is Mighty has done to me great things; and holy is His Name." Great words! (Luke 1:38-49) In the midst of all the adversity, Mary chose to bask in her blessings.

We all enjoy Mary's response. That was a great testimony of what the Lord had done in her life. It's like what happens after you have received the baptism of the Holy Spirit. Do you see the excitement here? Mary went off in the Spirit. She could not contain herself. She did not go off boasting, as if it was because of her holiness that God chose her. She chose to glorify the name of God. In her mind it was all about what LORD had done.

People of faith make very risky and surprising decisions. Abraham did the same thing. The three Hebrew young men did a similar thing to get into that fire. Faith does not make sense, because at that point she was no longer operating in the realm of the natural. No earthly and rational person would make such a decision. Faith stood above the disgrace, and the mockery. The most important thing for us was that all our lives depended on her decision. She came through for all of us.

THE BIRTH OF A KING

Nothing has ever happened, such as was about to take place nearly two thousand years since the King of the Universe was born. Angels have never celebrated anything at any time, and anywhere like it. We have seen that from the beginning they brought the news about His birth, and on this day, they celebrated in such a way that has never been done before. That morning a single angel broke the sky before the shepherds and declared in a very, very loud voice which might have been heard from Cleveland, Ohio to Los Angeles, California:

> **"Fear not, for behold I bring you good tidings of great joy which will be to all people. For unto you is born this day, in the city of David a Savior, who is Christ the Lord."** (Luke 2:10-11)

With those words the sky lit up even more with the glory of God, as a multitude, (probably millions) of the heavenly hosts (God's angelic military) descended on Bethlehem in probably a deafening, and thunderous praise, saying:

> **"Glory to God in the highest, and on earth, Peace and good will toward men."** (Luke 2:14)

Have you ever seen or heard a million-man choir sing? If you haven't, let me help you. The angelic choir might have been heard from Jerusalem to Nazareth. And people would have come from all over to see that mighty angelic choir. The Bible does not say it quite this way, but I am trying to let you see what a tremendous celebration that was. It was beyond words.

ANGELIC HOSTS

The bible says as soon as the angel of the Lord announced the birth of the Lord: "suddenly there was with the angel a multitude of the heavenly hosts with the angel praising God and saying, glory to the God in the Highest and on earth good will toward men." (Luke 2:13-14) These were not your regular angels, if I may call it that. They were special military angels known as angelic hosts. No description is given of them. We don't know if they wore uniforms or not, but we see a huge difference here. It's not every day that you see angels celebrating birthdays here on earth. It was really some type of celebration! That tells us about two things:

(1) a special celebration for a special Person, a King. (2) The presence of angelic hosts meant that heaven was prepared for anything that men might try to pull. History shows that the Roman Empire remained in peace for the thirty-three and a half years that He was on earth.

We see that through the death of king Herod who tried to murder the baby Jesus right after He was born. His servants had to intervene, appearing to Joseph and instructing him to take the baby to Egypt and back after the king died. They made sure that Baby Jesus was protected the whole time. They kept watch night and day.

Imagine a million-man angelic choir praising God. It must have sounded like a million voices. Oh! Before I forget, there was the glory of God that filled the skies! The shepherds might have thought the sky was going to fall on them. I am sure the sight was awesome. As the angelic choir slowly vanished into heaven the recovering shepherds woke each other up with the words, "let us go and see what the Lord has done." (Luke 2:15)

I had the opportunity of watching the Navy Band sing Christmas carols this past Christmas. Then I said to myself, "Imagine the angelic choir of that first Christmas! Imagine how their glorious voices might have sounded." It sent chills through my spine all over again. It was a glorious sight.

The Lord was born in glorious fashion, and Scripture says He grew in wisdom and in the Spirit of God. With the passage of time He went on to preach and teach the Great gospel of God to all people. Israel had very mixed notions about Him, and even today some unbelievers continue to subject us to the same treatment that the Lord went through. The controversy has gotten worse, especially in these last days, which prompts the question who is Christ?

THE CHRIST

This name is the Greek word for the anointed One of God, or the Messiah. What was He anointed for? I believe that (Isaiah 61:1-9) spells out what that anointing was. He was a Special Individual. He looked like every single one of us, but when He spoke, or did something people saw a different kind of person. People had read about Him for centuries, but when He came those who believed were not disappointed.

He was also the Savior of the world. Are we waiting for God, who is the Christ, the people asked and wondered? The answer is very simple for us now, but the Man who came was never expected, because God became a man just like us. People talked about God all their lives, they were taught about Him all their lives, but they had never seen Him. So, when He stood there looking like us, it was a hard pill to swallow. Nobody in the history of the world expected God to become a man the way Christ did. People wondered: "how could God be like one of us, I mean look at Him?" This Incarnate deity was the same God of the universe, and He proved it.

Here's the thing, they knew that God could do anything, but refused to see Him here as such, so the man they saw caused quite a stir. Among Satan's followers, he was just another man who would go the way of other men, meaning He could be tricked and in the end, die. He turned out to be devil-stumping, and demons would say, "What do you want with us, Son of God? Have you come to torture us before our time?" Israel would have learnt from demons Who Christ was. (Matthew 8:29)

Among the Lord's disciples the idea of the incarnation was just as strange. Confusion abounded, a situation that was to hound Him the rest of His time on earth. Well, God knew that. The song of the angels at His glorious birth was what I call the Gloria: "Glory to God in the highest, and on earth peace, good will toward men." (Luke 2:14) was exactly what God sent as a solution to the world. This song was a song of introduction, welcoming Him as Son of the Highest, heaven coming to the earth. It spelt out part of His mission to bring peace and good will toward all men.

The coming of the Lord was like a bomb dropped into the earth. For Satan and his followers, He was viewed as a thorn in their flesh the One Who came to bring an end to their reign. You could tell demons were on edge everywhere He showed up. They trembled at His presence, but the devil did not quite understand why Christ came (see Chapter 9). Satan played cool, thinking He would go the way of other men, but again he had totally misunderstood the mission of the Holy One.

Taking human form was also confusing to humans. Remember no human being has ever seen God even today. He was their first encounter with God, yet He was exactly like every human being, except that He was the same God they had been worshiping. That was very difficult to understand. Many wanted to see God very badly, but here He comes looking exactly like one of them. They could not believe it. They forgot that if the Christ, the God-man came in His true form they would not be able to see Him, because He would be spirit. Yet He was the exact person they needed.

Christ is the most controversial Figure ever known, and arguments about Him continue till this day. All of us have heard of God, but who that God was remained a mystery since the dawn of history. Many believe that God was perhaps some cosmic being that did not want to have anything to do with us. Others with the help of the devil still believe that God does not exist at all. For others God is like a landlord who built a house (the earth), and went away for good, because he just could not deal with the problems of managing His own creation. For those who study the sciences, based on what they have studied, they just cannot understand how one single Individual can create this vast and complex universe. That's why He is God.

For some in Israel when the angel brought the news about the coming of Christ no one could figure out what form He would take. It was bad enough that He took human form, but the question became what would He grow into? Some thought He would grow into a new King David, Solomon, or one of those past kings. So, as He walked the earth, and did things that only God could do (miracles), the intellectuals of His day (Pharisees, and Sadducees) still looked down on Him. So, Christ coming the way He did, became more of a problem than the solution that He was meant to be.

He was not that great of a man, because He was not handsome. The devil knew Who He was, but he never understood why He came, because he never knew that there was a Resurrection. Some people were content that God remained in the Galaxies, and so when He showed up the way He did it confirmed their unbelief. That's why scripture says Chris is the wisdom and the power of God.

What does the song signify in the overall scheme of things in the life of the Messiah? A brief history of Israel might shed some light. Before He was born Rome was on the neck of Israel, and the people were at each other's throat. The whole world was like an ocean gone wild. The song of the angels fitted very well with His mission of peace on earth. He was the Prince of the peace that the people desperately needed. When He calmed the storms that ought to have told them Who this Mighty Man was, mightier than the seas and the waves, and Israel's problems. Amen. (Mark 4:35-39)

Not only could He do what we just saw, but He brought peace in the hearts of men, where there was so much turmoil. With His Love He brought good will to men. Not just peace in times of peace but He taught us that you could have peace during the storms of life. The angels rejoiced because what the world truly needed was not more money, and material possessions, but the Christ of God who was also the answer to this big question of His looks. Scripture says:

> **"He had neither form nor beauty:**
> **When we shall see Him, He had no**
> **Beauty, that we should desire Him."** (Isaiah 53:2)

Before He was born, nobody knew what He would look like. You know we men like to admire appearances: how tall he is, how big he is, and how broad are his shoulders. This is what defines handsomeness. But Christ was not any of these. Scripture tells us that He was not a handsome Man. So, His very appearance was a big disappointment to many. If he looked tall, and big, He would have weighed better in our eyes. God knew that, and He would not send us the Person we esteemed. He was not an imposing Figure. He was not One who would stand out in a crowd; or One who would draw any kind of attention. I am not saying that He was an ugly guy, but He was not a wow-guy. God knew exactly what He was doing, because if He had sent an imposing guy He would have become an idol. You know how we humans are! We want to see a tall guy, well-shaped features, blue eyes, really a good-looking fellow, but God sent a Person Who was just the Right Guy. That's why even till today, they have Him looking the way we would have Him look: long hair, handsome, blue eyes, and so on. The guy you see on photographs in some denominations is nothing close to what Christ was.

From a book I read years ago called, "The greatest Story ever told," Christ was a stout, strong man, average build, and people quickly rejected Him. That's why Scripture says, "He was despised and rejected by men." You know how photos of angels look so beautiful, and handsome, but Christ was not an angel either.

Those of us who are Christians with the help of the Holy Spirit, we know Him as the very God that we have been waiting for. We identified with the signs He gave us that He is the all-powerful, all knowing, all-seeing, omnipresent One, etc. When you have power such as God does, doubters forget that He can do anything He wants, including coming to us as a human being.

Even for the astute theologians, one of the things we keep questioning in Christianity is the concept of Trinity. Scripture teaches that these designations came about through the concept of submission. All the parts of God: Father, Son and Spirit submit to each other and become one even though they can also function independently. Confusing, isn't it? God created us in the same way: with a soul, spirit, and body. The difference is our parts cannot function independently as God does. What I am getting at is that in taking human form Christ was exercising that dependence. In doing so He simply submitted His will to His Father. You hear Him say over and over, "I have not come to do MY own will, but to do the will of My Father." He is the same God that we have heard of since time began.

SON OF GOD

Christ is the Son of God. That means He is God fully. He was declared to be the Son, because He preexisted with the Father and created all things, before time began. He was not a son through human procreation, because the Father had no wife. At Bethlehem He came forth of the Holy Spirit, so Joseph was not His father. See Son described above.

SON OF MAN

Christ is the Son of Man. That means He was fully man like every single one of us. He had a body, a soul, and a spirit. The difference is He had never sinned, and He was born of the Holy Spirit. He also had flesh and blood. Another difference is His blood was pure and powerful, because He was sinless. His blood had cleansing power. As a man His blood was the only blood that could take away all sin. That's why He was also called the Lamb of God. (John 1:29)

You see Him in the manger He looked like another ordinary and a human child. He could feel pain, could feel tired, and could feel love. He was limited in terms of the fact that he could not be in many places at the same time. He was truly God in the flesh. At the same time when you saw Him calm the storms, rebuke a tree and it died, walk on water, raise the dead, heal all manner of diseases, feed thousands with little or nothing, He did the things that only God could do. When devils sensed His presence, they trembled and felt threatened, you knew this was an Extraordinary Individual.

The parables or stories He told contained such wisdom that the world had never known. Theologians of His day marveled about His wisdom! They asked is this not the son of Joseph, which institution of higher learning did He graduate from. He taught with such amazing clarity and simplicity. People came from all over to listen to Him speak. As He taught He made complex biblical statutes appear simple.

His personality was magnetic and soothing. His presence was the place to be, because His peace calmed weary souls. People suspended or rearranged their schedules to come and hear Him speak. Some listened for days, and days, but could not have enough of His teachings. His words lifted them up to new heights, and brought them to higher realms of life, and they knew this was the King of Glory. Through His teachings people felt they could reach out and touch the very throne of God, and they knew He was the Son of the living God.

He was a loving Father, and a Brother. He loved everyone, and no matter what anybody did or looked like they were welcome. He spent His days with them, and they could not get enough of Him. His words like: "come unto me all ye who labor and are heavy-laden and I will give you rest," were like music to the ears of millions of hearers, and weary souls. They drew multitudes upon multitudes. At some point He had to speak to them from a boat taken from one of His disciples. He gave food to the hungry, life to the sick and dying, and everybody who came received something. He spent the nights, and days among His crowds, and He told them, "foxes have holes, and birds of the air have nests, but the Son of Man had no place to lay His head." (Luke 9:56) This was truly a description of a Man who had no home and made His home among His crowds. He was in Galilee today and in Judea tomorrow. He was so busy to the extent He had no time for Himself, and His disciples wondered: "did He have anything to eat? But no matter how busy he got He always found time to pray, teaching us the most valuable lesson: "that we must always pray no matter how busy we get." The Son of man had given His soul to the ones He had come to save.

His heart was with the sheep that the Father had given Him, and He remarked at some point that: "anyone who came to Him, He will at no wise cast out." He was the Good Shepherd, who gave His life for His sheep. One day, consumed with the work He almost ignored His mother and brothers. Pointing to the crowds He asked: "Who are my mother and brothers? Whoever does the will of my Father is my mother, my brothers and my sisters." (Mark 3:33-34) His family understood because they knew that He had to do the work that Father had given Him. At the end of His life here on earth He died alone provided it pleased the Father that He had finished the task, as He uttered His last words: "it is finished." (John 19:30). What a Savior!

INDWELLING SPIRIT

Christ is the Indwelling Spirit known as the Holy Spirit. He has the power to indwell us. In doing that, He shaped us into the image of Christ. He told the disciples these words: "Even the Spirit of Truth whom the world cannot receive because they do not know Him shall be in you." (John 14:17) He was the only One who could give us His Spirit, and that is what guarantees our salvation. Without the Spirit of God no one could be saved.

Before He rose He told the disciples that after He went to the Father He would send the Holy Spirit to indwell them. At that point He was no longer limited. He became omnipresent and could live in all of us. He would live in us to teach, mold, and shape us into Christ and to empower us to do the work of His kingdom. No one else could give the Spirit of God to anyone, except Him. Many things could not be done unless He went to the Father to send the Spirit to His followers.

IMPLICATIONS FOR DIVINITY

The woman at the well said to Him, "I know that MES-SIAH cometh which is called Christ: when He comes He will teach us all things." (John 4:25) The Lord answered, "I that is speaking unto thee am He." (John 4:26) Nobody knows all things except God. The lady was telling Him that the Messiah is their God, the One who knows all things pertaining to life. He sees all things and knows all things. In this same chapter, the Scripture says, He told the woman of her past and present life. Christ was the all-wise God.

He came to help us with the same matters of life. The woman, like most of us, loved God, and as we saw in that chapter, she did not know how to worship and to live for God. Christ came to teach us that "true worshippers would worship in spirit and in truth." (John 4:25-26)

She lived a religious life which was not pleasing to God. She was living a polygamous life, and like us He told her in a nonjudgmental way that it was not right. He taught her that He knew her, and her life. No wonder the woman went and told her people to come and see a Man who told her about all the things that she had ever done. He knew her past, present and future. He knows ours too. We can't hide from the all-seeing eyes of God. The ability for Christ to know the past and future pointed to His divinity.

ALL-WISE GOD

Christ was also omniscient. Day after day the Pharisees and Sadducees sought to trap him. They read through their law books, but they could not catch Him. All they had to do was watch His activities to understand that He was Israel's Messiah, but even that too failed. After the Lord healed the man born blind they accused him of not keeping the Sabbath saying: "This man is not from God, for He does not keep the Sabbath," and totally missing the point" (John 9:16) Even the onlookers said, "how could a sinner do such miraculous signs? Their power was in the law, but even that got them all confused, to the extent that a blind man could see that the Lord was their Messiah.

THE LORD

At His birth the angel said, "Unto to you is born in the city of David, which is **Christ, The LORD**." (Luke 2:11) I love that statement. Two titles given to Him at His birth described Him as Christ and Lord. We have been discussing Christ as the Messiah. In this section we shall be looking as the title of Lord. The word Lord means the Creator, the Owner, or Possessor, Ruler, Emperor, and ELOHIM.

Abram found that out in Genesis 14:19 when he said, "I am El-ELYON, the Possessor of heaven and earth." He created all things, owns all things, He is the One to whom service is due. Everyone who lives in heaven and on earth must know that they belong to Him, and they owe Him everything. Whether you know it or not we all owe Him service. We owe Him our lives: everything we own, the air we breathe, belongs to the Lord.

As OWNER, He owns all things, both visible and invisible. There are two ways of ownership: (1) creation, and (2) purchase. All things belong to him, because He created them. He is the true owner. When you purchase something you own it, but that kind or ownership is only temporary. The temporary nature of possession is for two reasons: (1) the purchaser is merely leasing, and (2) The lessee does not live forever. The true owner is the Creator who lives forever. Therefore, Christ is Lord.

Creation is not about owning things that exist, but it is originating and bringing into existence things which have not existed before. It also means giving life to things that have never existed. Scripture says

God spoke things into being saying, "Let there be light, let there be the expanse, and the world came into being." (Genesis 1:3) In the process God gave life to previous deadness. That's creation. Before Him there was no creator, and after Him there will be no Creator. Nobody can create even a grain of soil.

For anyone to create they must be able to step out of this universe and create theirs. A scientist may turn dirt into white or red, but the basic understanding is that it is still dirt, created by the Creator. That scientist is not a creator he is a scientist who did not create the things he is mixing. There's only One Creator, and that is the Lord Jesus Christ.

THE POWER TO CREATE:

Everybody cannot just speak, and things happen. That takes tremendous power. God is a Supernatural, and Incomprehensible Being. He has no beginning, and no end, therefore, He is Incomprehensible. His ways are past understanding. Yes, He created all: it says: "the heavens declare the glory of God; the skies display His hand-work. Day unto day utters speech, and night unto night reveals knowledge. There is no speech, nor language where their voice is not heard. Their line has gone out through all the earth and their words to the end of the world." (Psalm 19:1-4) The heavens show His power.

POWER TO SUSTAIN

The Lord also sustains. Scripture says His work is on display for the world to see: "the heavens declare the glory of God." (Psalm 19:1) That is our God. It also says, "He upholds everything with the word of His mouth." If you look at the earth you wonder: how does the sky hang up there or how do the oceans not over flood the lands? That is because the Lord sustains everything. He has the power to do that. Therefore, creation is not complete until the Creator can sustain it.

LORD also means Ruler or Emperor. He is the King of kings, and the Lord of lords. He is both above all those who call themselves kings, or lords. All the kings of the earth are under His leadership. It's like an Emperor over all minor kings in the empire. He provides counsel to all minor kings. They call Him Lord. We know that He Lords over our souls conforming them into Himself, until we become a perfect man attaining to the measure, and the fullness of Christ.

We know that He will physically establish His kingdom on this earth and will physically rule someday. We need a King who knows all things, upon whom the government shall be on His shoulders. Nothing escapes His sight, and true justice will reign, true peace shall fill the earth. The songwriter states: "joy to the world the Savior reigns…" joy, peace, and righteousness will fill the earth. According to that song we are moving to the day when this will happen. That's the way He created it, and we cannot wait!

Lord means Master meaning the One to Whom, service is due, or owed. One of the things we must do on this earth is to serve Him. God did not send us into this world to do our own thing, but to serve Him. He knows all things, He owns all things, and we owe Him His service. We are not here to have a good time, to just have fun our own way, but to do things His way. Make sure that whatever you are doing you are doing what He has planned for you to do.

There are so many things that the Lord has done for us. First, He has given us life. Without Him there will be no life for every single one of us. You think about it and you'd see that we owe Him even ourselves. And then you ask the question: why are we here and what does He want us to do for him? In my first book, "THE POWER OF FAITH," I pondered these things. If you think about it you will see that we are not good people, because in everything we do we always need His help. I remember asking Him about my ex-wife getting sick, and I thought what about all that I have done for You Lord? And He said: "you have not done anything. I am the One who did everything through you. The scripture He gave me says: "In Him we live, we move, and we have our being." (Acts 17: 28)

The Lord is not asking for much from us. He wants that we should always have Him in our hearts, so that we can "Love, worship, and serve Him." In these three things He has already done the two for us. He has loved us, and He has served us. He loved us so much He came to earth and took human flesh. In serving us He gave His own life for us. There remains only one thing: We must worship Him.

Christ is "ELOHIM – JEHOVAH, the LORD God, Almighty, who is, Who Was, and Is to come. (Luke 2:11I, Isaiah 9:6) These words mean He has always been. He is in the past, and Is now, and He is in the Future. How is that? We cannot explain. He is the "Incomprehensible." He created all things and gave life to all things. "Without Him there was nothing that was made."

The name Jehovah is a compound name of God. It describes who God is; as for example the God of Peace, the God of all Power, etc. Jehovah-JIREH, Jehovah-NISSI, and Jehovah Shalom, translated as the God peace.

THE PRINCE OF PEACE

Christ is the Prince of Peace. That is the power of God through Christ, to create, or manufacture a soothing peace in unstable times. That is because He is the prince or author of peace. The bible says, "He Himself is our peace, who has broken down the middle wall of separation." (Ephesians 2:14). According to this His peace always seems to break down separation and brings people together. He did that between Peter and Matthew. These two were arch enemies, but they were brought together, and when they saw each other in His presence, they simply broke down and confessed. They knew that this was not the place to live in separation. His presence is a place for the cessation of war. They became brothers from then on. What a Savior!

Peace is not just calmness it is a fruit of the Spirit of God. In other words, it is a spirit. It is the power of God that creates calm even when conditions are in turmoil. There's no need for a child of God to be capricious during a bad situation, knowing that God is in control. When life is tumultuous He is the peace of God which passes understanding, which guards our hearts and minds through Christ Jesus. His peace rules in our hearts and brings that calmness when things go beyond our control, helping us to make the right choices when things fall apart. It is what separates us from the unbelieving world, for a child of God must have the power to operate in His peace.

You can sense the peace of Christ in those who have been filled with His Spirit. His peace helps us to be collected so we can act diligently. Peace like a river that covers the earth in His presence. It is what makes life better. One day He was in the boat with His disciples, and a big storm arose, and He quickly went to sleep. The boat was tossed up and down, and the waves were out of control. The twelve disciples were frightened: "Master, we perish," they screamed. When He woke up He spoke to the waves: "**Peace, be still**," and the storm died down in a hissing sound: "SH-SH-HHH-HHHHH-HHHHHH-HHHH-OOOO-SSSSSS!" in obedience to the mighty command of the Prince of Peace. And peace was restored.

CHAPTER 3

Angels - Who They Are

MAL'AKH

The first creations of the Lord Jesus Christ were spiritual beings called MAL'AKH, or angels. We know that because the Lord created heaven and all the spiritual beings in it before humans. (Colossians 1:16) He created all things, visible and invisible. The invisible creations are all types of angelic beings. The word MAL'AKH is the Hebrew for messenger, or ambassador. Messenger is used one hundred and eleven times in the King James Version of the Holy Bible, and ambassador, ninety- eight times. (Hebrews 1:7)

Another name for an angel is "I am sent." (Daniel. 10:11) When Gabriel appeared to Daniel in the Old Testament, and to Mary, in the New Testament, he used the phrase "I am sent," giving us yet another name for Messenger. God is not like anyone anywhere, so He created special supernatural beings to do His work. Angels are these supernatural beings who carry God's messages and do other services required by the Almighty. When I say the Almighty, I mean God, and when I speak of God I mean God the Father, the Son, and the Holy Spirit. I will be using the Lord Jesus Christ in that capacity throughout this book.

The story of God can be a little complicated. Most people know God through their religion, but no one has ever seen Him. The coming of Jesus Christ has made the story much more confusing. It caught me by surprise, because people were not expecting God to be a human being. Angels came to report the coming of the great Savior, but they also came to be witnesses of His Majestic Incarnation. They celebrated His birth, they were with Him during His life and ministry, they were the first on Resurrection Day, they announced His Second Coming and they were involved in the start of the New Church. The presence of angels shows us that there was a heavenly presence during the Incarnation.

The subject of angels is difficult to understand, because we see them as humans, then the bible tells us that they are spirits. The truth is they are not human at all. The first encounter with angels is when Satan came to tempt Adam and Eve in Eden, the Garden of God. Lucifer as he was called then showed up as a serpent, or snake. Other Biblical accounts of angels reveal them as beasts having many eyes, gentlemen having wings, young men as farmers, and then mighty beings of war.

SPIRITUAL BEINGS

The word angel means wind, or spirit or material being. They may appear as human to us, but they have no material bodies. Scripture tells us that holy angels are the sons of God, but fallen angels are followers of the devil. (Jude 1:6) That's why as a Christian we rely on the Holy Spirit who helps us concerning spirits, because fallen angels may sometimes disguise as angels of light. The subject of evil angels will be discussed in the next chapter, but our focus in this entire book is on holy angels.

Scripture also says, "God makes His ministers flame of fire, who do His bidding." (Hebrew 1:7; Psalm 104:4). This is probably because of the energy they have, and the speed at which they serve. Fire is very active agent and angels are very active, and always on the move.

Angels do not have to go through the birth and growth process as we humans do. They were created one day as grown-ups and they knew every-thing that God wanted them to know. They were created as males therefore thy do not procreate. There are those who think that they have the potential to procreate, there's no biblical evidence that they can procreate. There are no older and baby-angels. They come to us transformed as young men, old men or middle-aged, but there are no old or young angels. They have lived for billions of years, but they do not grow old. They are therefore ageless.

No one has ever seen an angel approaching in the distance. That is because they always appear and disappear. They travel at the rate of thought. That is why an angel can travel from heaven to earth in one moment. (Daniel 9:21) This verse shows that the prophet needed information, and an angel was dispatched from heaven, but by the time Daniel turned around the angel was there. It's like from heaven all the LORD had to do is call the city, or country, and the angel is there. Generally, their rate of travel is incalculable by human means.

Angels are supernatural beings whose existence, appearances, and activities are not explainable by natural means. That means some of what they do are above anything natural. That also means the laws of physics do not apply to them. They come from a higher realm of existence much higher than our own. For example, they can transform into humans, but we cannot transform into anything. Their power is unexplainable, and their strength is above that of human technologies and machines. All we know is their source of power and strength is God.

Unless they transform to humans, scripture does not show any interaction between humans and angels. I have never read anything about humans and angels shaking hands, or hugging. The present CORINA-virus has revealed how germy we humans really are. Facts show that we have transmitted diseases to each other for centuries. Even if we could hug angels, they are holy, and cannot be infected. When they transform into humans we still cannot approach them because the power of holiness protects them. The closest we have seen is humans receiving messages from angels and that is only when they let us. Even at that point they are usually too powerful for us. The bottom line is angels are not our friends, in the sense of human relationships, so we cannot approach them even if we wanted to. They are our spiritual brethren though.

Scripture also says that angels are messengers of God and the Lord Jesus Christ. God created them more like Himself, which is to say spirit. They are made far superior to man, and we shall see why. Since their creation they have lived with Him in heaven. That means they were all recreated holy, because God is holy. No one knows when they were created except God. As we saw earlier, after Adam and Eve were created it was the first time that humans met with this angelic being known as Satan. He had been around for ages like other supernatural beings, yet most of us know very little or nothing about them. Our limited knowledge of them has spun all kinds of tales about angels. The goal of this book is to clarify some of the myths about angels. Our sources are completely biblical.

The word angel has been thrown around so much so that people think every good person is an angel, but that is not true. That statement is only partly true, because there are evil angels too. If you watch movies you will be surprised at what you see concerning these amazing creatures. From movies I learned that when humans die they turn into angels in the next life, acquiring supernatural powers able to right the wrongs of their previous life. This may be a good story for movies, but it is totally false. We will discuss more of these fallacies in the sections below.

FALLACIES ABOUT ANGELS

The term fallacy means a false belief about something. Conventional belief says that angels are these delicate, beautiful, and feminine creatures, flying around purposelessly. None of that is true. Some of the fallacies come even from believers themselves. ANGELIC WITNESS is committed to bringing out the truth about angels as contained in the Holy Scriptures.

There is the belief that when people die they become angels and serve God. That is false. God has created an innumerable number of angels to serve Him. He does not need dead humans who appoint themselves as God's servants. The truth is humans cannot do the work of angels, and there is no such need in heaven or anywhere.

Again, humans cannot become angels and vice versa. He does not need people who appoint themselves as His servants who are not equipped to do the work of angels. God has created us to serve Him here on earth, and the first man failed miserably. If we can't do well on our own earth how are we going to do elsewhere?

Many are led to believe that men and women are angels somewhere out of this life. That is also false. There is only heaven and the earth. Heaven is for spiritual beings, and the earth is for humans. There are no other habitable planets elsewhere. We know that because when Satan was cast out of heaven his next destination was the earth. When he finally exits the earth, he will be hell-bound. That will be great for all of us.

Sometimes we are concerned about what would happen to our family members, namely husbands, wives, and children. The Lord explained the question of marriage when asked this question: "as family members took turns as husbands of a deceased brother, who will then be the next husband in heaven?" He said, "You will be as the holy angels in heaven not giving and taking into marriage." (Matthew 22:29-30) There will be no men, and women in heaven, and there will be no more marriages there either. The Lord Jesus then confirmed the genderless issue of angels too.

Another fallacy is angels being portrayed as delicate feminine creatures. Those are not angels at all. They are just human beings posing as angels. Angels have no gender, so they are neither male nor female, but they are addressed as male. They are the most powerful, and fearless creatures, on the face of the entire universe. They speak for God, and they act as directed by the LORD. They perform miracles without having to pray and hand out judgments when necessary. Their movement is completely planned, and strategic, according to the will of the Almighty God.

Most people believe that all angels have wings. That's not accurate based on biblical accounts on the subject. I know that in the Book of Daniel where Gabriel is seen flying, not all angels have wings. In the Book of Ezekiel and the Book of Revelation we see Cherubim and Seraphim with wings. CHERUBIM have four wings and Seraphim have six. It seems clear to me that whether they have wings or not depends on the decision of the Almighty One. If He wants all or none of them to have wings, the decision will be His. Among some Christians, cherubim are mere symbolic representations of some character of God. That is also erroneous. Cherubim are powerful angels of God who are some of the closest to Him. They cover the mercy seat and God sits between them in the Arch of the Covenant. (Ezekiel. 1:1-29; Luke 1:26) We also know that they are real angels, because the LORD referred to Lucifer as the anointed- Cherub before he fell from grace. The LORD God said, "You are the anointed cherub that covers." (Ezekiel. 28:14) Lucifer was Satan's original name, and I believe that he was not the only cherub.

Yet another fallacy says that all people have guardian angels. What we call guardian angels is what Scripture calls ministering spirits sent forth to minister to them who shall be heirs of salvation. Holy angels are God's servants sent forth to minister to those who are, and those who would be heirs of Salvation, and not to every human being. God loves the world, but if you have not received Christ you cannot have a guardian angel. Those who may receive angelic assistance include innocent little children, according to the Lord Jesus. Remember also that all angels are not holy, and the unholy angels do not represent God. They represent Satan, and Satan does not help anyone. He wants to kill, not help. We also know that all people are created by God, but all people are not the children of God. The term children of God are the redeemed. God sent the Lord Jesus Christ to bring salvation to all humans, and when you fail to believe in Christ God will not send His angel to be your guardian angel.

Note, if you are not saved right now, there's still room at the cross for you. God wants all of us to be His children, but that happens only when you receive Jesus Christ as your Savior. You can confess your sins and receive Him into your heart right now. Pray this prayer adopted from Jimmy SWAGGART Ministries,

> **"Oh God in heaven I come to You now in the name of Jesus; I am sorry for my sins; the life I have lived; the wicked things I have done; with my mouth I confess the Lord Jesus; in my heart I believe that God raised Him from the dead; I believe that He is alive; and that I have been washed; and I am cleansed. Today I make Him the Lord of my life; and I am saved. I will serve Him the rest of my days; In Jesus name I pray, amen."**
> (Romans 10:9)

ORIGINS OF ANGELS

No one knows when angels were created, but the bible tells us that they were created in the ions of time by our Lord Jesus Christ who created all things, both visible and invisible; be they dominions, or thrones were all created by Him and for Him, and without Him was not anything made that was made. (John 1:3) As mentioned above He made them for Himself as His servants, with immeasurable strength meant to serve Him in any way He pleased.

Angels were not made the same way as human. Sources say they were all made on the same day. They were made without gender, and their numbers were predetermined by God. They were made with extraordinary strength, and according to their hierarchies. The main differences between humans and angels are angels are not made to reproduce after their own kind, and they were not made to rule over their own universe.

The Lord is their King, and as King he possesses them just as He possesses all things in the universe. They have tremendous wisdom and knowledge, and I am not saying that they are omniscient. Scripture says, "They know all things in the earth." (2 Samuel. 14:20) As their King, they go where He goes, and they serve Him where He wants them to. When the Lord walked the earth, His angels were with Him, and they heard everything He taught. Their answers on Resurrection Day prove that. (Matthew 28:6)

God made His angels spirit like Himself and they have been there for billions of years. As He spoke of the regeneration of time when He will come again to set up His throne, they will be there to serve Him until the consummation when He will finally judge the world and put the man of sin away for good. Angels are not God's helpers; it is their duty to serve Him as their King and Lord forever and ever.

He has called them reapers, gathers all made to serve Him. Angels are not given independent power to roam the universe, to be their own gods, or have relationships with anybody they please. So, fallacies that say angels get women pregnant are false, and ignorant. Their abode is in heaven, a place which is by comparison higher and better than the earth, specifically at the throne of the Most- High God, where they behold His face, to learn of His will. The incomparable riches of heaven leave no room for any angels to desire to live on earth.

HOLINESS

God **alone** is holy, and those He chooses to share His holiness with. He does so with His angels. The Lord Jesus referred to them as His holy angels many times. That's also the difference between the angels of God and fallen angels. The holiness of God means four things: (1) He is unique, (2) He is sovereign; (3) He is light, and He is pure and perfect. Uniqueness means there's no one in the universe like Him. He stands alone.

God's sovereignty means He alone sets the rules upon which the universe operates. God is light means He dwells eternally in the light. That means He is light. He is perfect means His perspective is always right. The holiness of God also means He is pure. That means He is pristine, incorruptible, or undefiled.

Angels are holy, because God is holy. Without Him they have no holiness of their own. The angels do not have the same holiness as the LORD. For example, they don't have the attributes that God has. They are not unique, they are not sovereign, they are not the light, and they are not perfect. He shares His holiness with His angels, as He shares His glory too. Angels stand before God in heaven which is where they live. When Gabriel came to Zacharias, the priest he said, "I am Gabriel I stand before God." According to Dr. Jacque Graham's Book on angels, he said angels spend their time around the throne of God learning about the will of God. It gives me the impression that there's much to be studied around the person of God, and there's no book large enough to contain all information about the Almighty. There is enough to keep us studying forever and ever.

Even angels cannot stand in the light of God. That's why they cover their faces in the presence of God, because the brightness of the light is so powerfully bright that they cannot look directly at Him. That light shines through all things. Night and day are the same to Him. No evil can hide around Him. That's why the devil could not hide with his evil plan of overthrowing the Mighty One.

TYPES OF ANGELS

There are two groups of angels: holy angels of God, and evil angels. All angels are not servants of God, and do not serve or represent the LORD. Holy angels live and serve God, but evil angels were cast out of heaven because of their rebellion. These evil angels serve Satan. Other angels are confined in the abyss, and if you ask me they are not angels at all. Satan and his angels can disguise as angels of light, but they do not serve God, so you do not want anything to do with them. The word light signifies goodness, purity, and holiness, associated with God only. They disguise themselves, because they are anything but light. They do not help anyone, and they have come to kill, steal, and destroy you, your friends, and families. We will discuss their mission in detail in the next chapter, but our goal in this book is to discuss holy angels who serve God, and the brethren of the redeemed.

CLOTHED WITH GLORY

When I speak of the glory of God I am speaking of divine splendor, holiness, magnificent perfection, character and manifested righteousness, brightness, power, and His surpassing greatness. There are really no words in our vocabulary to describe who God is. He is so great that He has extended that glory to some of His servants, His holy angels. (Psalm 19:1)

Holy angels have a radiance around them which stands for purity, perfection, and power. This radiance is what is called the glory of God. That glory is like a special covering, aura, or anointing, visibly manifested on all the angels of God. The glory of God is also the power of God. That is what makes it impossible for humans to come near them. No human being is powerful enough to approach an angel unless he allows them to. When the prophet Daniel saw the angel Gabriel, he became practically dead. Usually no flesh can mix with anything holy. Angels are holy, but we are sinful. That's what prevents us from approaching them. Their presence overwhelms any flesh. It is really like light and darkness. They are the light, and we are the darkness. When light runs into darkness it consumes it. So, it is what happens when angels come around anything flesh.

Satan and his demons are not sons of God. They do not also have the glory, and so they do not have the power of God. They sinned against God, and therefore they are no longer sons of God. They do not live in heaven, because they are no longer holy. Satan and his demons do not even belong in the earth, but God allows Satan to settle in the earth, because He plans to use him for His purposes. Through Christ you and I have power over Satan, and all who confess Christ.

HIERARCHY OF ANGELS

There are about five orders of angels. You may read books that carry additional orders, but as far as the Holy Bible is concerned there are only those that we carry. This hierarchy does not translate into rankings. They are duties which they perform, for all angels are simply messengers and servants of the Most-High God. Biblical accounts reveal that these five orders are the following: Archangels, Angelic Hosts, Cherubim, Seraphim, and Guardian Angels. They are also called angelic powers.

Again, the term hierarchy r does not necessarily designate ranking or class, but it has to do with various offices that angels hold. These hierarchies are as follows:

1. ARCHANGELS

Among the angels of God archangels are the highest group. The word archangel means head or chief angel. We know that Michael is the star prince or head of all the angels. Again no one knows how many of them are there. Michael gets called to assist in the most serious spiritual battles against Satan's demons around the universe. He is the one who led the war against Lucifer to cast him out of heaven. That's leadership. Every angel looked up to him. (Jude 1:9; 1Thesolonians 4:16) It seems as if the seven angels who stand around the throne of God are also archangels, but there's no biblical reference to that.

The term archangel has been used only two times in the bible. In the first quote the Lord returns to earth for the Rapture with the shout and with the voice of the Archangel. This archangel will probably be Michael. He is so great that God uses his voice. In another reference the archangel Michael rebukes the devil over the body of Moses. Who else can be called to face Satan, but Michael? When it comes to heavy matters the archangel is always called in. Michael was also called to assist Gabriel in Daniel chapter 10. As we have seen in the book of Revelation angels are unbelievably mighty and incredibly powerful as they do the work of God's incredibly complex machine called heaven. We'll be discussing these mighty angels in subsequent chapters.

2. ANGELIC HOSTS

(Luke 2: 13)
Angelic hosts are God's military. They are those angels who have very fierce appearances. We see them in Daniel Chapter Ten (Michael), Luke Chapter Two, Matthew Chapter 28:2-6, and in the Book of revelation. I know with certainty that Michael is their leader. No one knows how many hosts are there, but we saw a very large contingent of them when the Lord was born in Bethlehem.

They are charged with warring against the enemies of God in the entire universe. The bible also shows that they fight against violators of the law of the Most-High God, whether spiritual or human. They also fight to protect the people of God in the kingdom of God here on earth. So, spiritual wars are always raging on around the universe. (See Daniel Chapter Ten.) They are very powerful, equipped from the massive and infinite reserves of the Almighty.

3. CHERUBIM

CHERUBIM of glory, so called because of their proximity to God. These angels are also called living creatures. Some of them have different kinds of appearances. In Ezekiel 1:1-29 they have four faces, and four wings. One face is that of an ox, the face of a man, the other is that of a lion, and the other like an eagle. They lift their two wings upward to cover the Mercy Seat, and the other two wings cover their bodies. They sit facing the Mercy Seat (above the Ark of Testimony. The LORD God meets between the two CHERUBIM which are on the Ark of the Testimony. (Ezekiel 28: 14)

They are the angels of covering, because they cover the Mercy Seat. They seem to be those who travel with the God of the universe. Wherever He goes they go. No name is given for these living creatures in Ezekiel, but in Ezekiel chapter twenty-eight the LORD called one of them a covering cherub when He was speaking to Lucifer:

> "You were the anointed cherub who covers
> You were on the holy mountain of God;
> You walked back and forth in the fiery stones." (Ezekiel 28:14)

In that address the LORD God also called Lucifer anointed. The LORD was addressing him on his last day. Lucifer is no longer anointed nor is he a covering angel. We shall discuss his fall in the next chapter as we look at evil angels. In the Jewish magazine, Angels in Judaism, there other cherub named Gabriel, URIEL, Raphael (Lucifer)

4. SERAPHIM OF GLORY

SERAPHIMS are also very close to His Glorious Majesty Himself, the Lord Jesus Christ the Lord of Glory. Out of the throne room in heaven come the four living Creatures having the following features: the first beast is like a lion; second beast is like a calf, the third like a man; and the fourth beast is like a flying eagle. Here's the difference: Seraphim each have six wings, while CHERUBIM have four. With two wings they cover their face, with two they cover their feet, and with two they fly. They cover their faces, because they can't face the light surrounding God's throne. No name was given to these beings. They are also full of eyes like the cherubim. They are named Seraphim in the Book of Isaiah. (Isaiah 6:3)

Seraphim are shown as worshippers of God as they cry:

"Holy, holy, holy;
The Lord God Almighty;
The whole earth is full of His glory!" (Isaiah 6:3)

As mentioned in Revelation chapter Four, day and night and forever and ever they don't stop praising saying holy, holy, holy, the LORD God Almighty. Imagine that. What power and energy! This is impossible with humans. That tells me how powerful angels are.

GUARDIAN ANGELS

(Hebrews 1:14)
Some angels are called guardian angels. These are those that are sent to protect people who are Christians. These are people who have received the Lord. That means the people who have totally given their heart to the Lord. Another way to say this is those people who have repented of their sins. Some people in the church today have not confessed their sins, and therefore are not saved. That also means these people have no guardian angels. God does not send His angels to protect people who have not given their heart to the Lord Jesus.

I am saying this because I want people to truly repent of their sins. Some people do not know or believe that they have sinned. If you are like that then Christ died in vain. God has sent His guardian angels to protect His children who have repented of their sins and have been forgiven by Christ. Whether you have seen your guardian angel or not my belief is that he is there, because Scripture says so. An angel of any type is a great help. Again, God may send an angel of any color. The decision is His.

As I mentioned earlier, people who have not been redeemed do not have guardian angels for that reason. You must be saved to have one, because children of God have guardian angels. Jesus Christ did not die to give every person a guardian angel. We must receive Christ and His salvation to become the children of God.

HISTORY OF ANGELIC ACTIVITY

Angels were introduced to man in Genesis chapter three, and soon after came the fall of man as the first couple sinned and were thrown out of the Garden. The one they saw was not the angel of God. He was Lucifer, the devil. We have been careful to explain to you the different types of angels because some do not particularly care about humans. You will know the right angel when you hear what he is telling you. If it is too good to be true, then it is not true. The best thing is to know the Word of God. If what the angel tells you does not line up with the Word, then he is not a holy angel.

After man fell, God deployed Cherubim to protect the Tree of Life. Therefore, the second angel seen by man was still a Cherubim, but the man could not tell the difference. The consequences of sin took away the power that God gave man, and God has continued to use angels to do His work in places where the man couldn't. They are usually called "the angel of the LORD," or "Angel of the LORD), referring to the Lord Jesus Christ Himself if the word angel is capitalized.

From the Genesis introduction, God's angels have been involved in all kinds of activities, side-by-side man both in the Old and New Testaments. They were fully involved in the Ministry of Christ during the first advent, but they laid low as the Master Himself was in full charge.

The whole bible is full of angelic activities: In the Book of Genesis the angel of the Lord brought the message to Hagar, Sarah's maid informing her to return to Sarah, and also gave her the name of her soon-to-be-born son Ismail; In Genesis 19:1-26, two angels destroyed Sodom and Gomorrah; Genesis 22:11-12, the angel of the Lord rescued Isaac, from his father's (Abraham) sharp knife; In Exodus 3:2, the angel of the Lord called on Moses from the Burning Bush; In Numbers 22:22-35, the angel of the Lord blocked Balaam's horse, as Balaam disobeyed God's command; 1 Chronicles 21:15, the angel of the Lord killed seventy thousand people, because of king David's disobedience; and there are tens of thousands of other references in the Old Testament concerning angelic activities.

ANGELS IN THE INCARNATION

Presidents and other heads of state are accompanied by their high military officials and other officials when they travel. When the Lord was about to come to earth His angels were the first to make the announcement. It was not an accident that the angels who came were God's own military: angelic hosts. Scripture stated: "Suddenly a large number of heavenly hosts appeared with the angel on that glorious morning." (Luke 2:13) They were with Him from His birth and remained until after they established the Church and took out the last enemy of the Church king Herod.

They heard the teachings that the Lord gave, they understood the commands. Below are verses of scripture that verified angelic presence during our Lord's Incarnation. Matthew 2:13 shows that Joseph was instructed to take the Baby to Egypt and 2:19 he was instructed to take the Child back to Nazareth. In Matthew angels ministered to the Lord after the temptation in the wilderness. Matthew chapter 13:30-49 the Lord taught the people on matters of life calling angels reapers, and harvesters in the end times. Matthew's gospel scripture shows part of the Lord's speech saying: "the gates of **hades** shall not prevail against it." (Matthew 16:18) Angels understood this to mean a command to take on the powers of darkness during the beginning of the church. The response by the angels was timely. Just when the backs of the apostles thought they were running out strength, reinforcements came in. The Leaders of Israel who thought the church was just a group of radicals out of Galilee were in for a big surprise. The angelic support quickly released to church to go back preaching in the temple.

In (Matthew 16:21, 20:19, and 26:32), the Lord mentioned that He was going to Jerusalem to be tormented and crucified and on the third day rise again. While the church went to sleep, the angels were the first on Resurrection morning. In Saint John gospel chapter 18:36, the Lord mentioned in the trial that He could summon His angelic fighters to fight against the Israeli government. Again, in Acts 1:11 angels announced the second coming of the Lord. In all these events angels showed up to do their part and they walked along with their King until His death.

ANGELIC POPULATION

How many angels are there? No number is listed anywhere in the bible and no one knows. Scripture tells us simply that they are innumerable or uncountable. Judging from the fact that Satan came to tempt the first couple when they were created shows that angels were created long before man. By His infinite wisdom God knew how many of them He would need from beginning to end. It is a simple mathematical problem for the Lord who is omniscient and who is the Alpha and the Omega.

We know that they do not procreate, and they do not die, and we are not told if their number increases periodically or not. Out of that original number, whatever that number is, one third of them was cast out of heaven because of their sin. Out of that number some of them were cast into hell, and some were chained and delivered in chains in darkness, reserved for the day of final judgment.

Even the number that remained after the routing of Satan and his followers are described as undetermined, or mathematically incalculable. By His power God created His angels without number for His mighty military system. The question of how many angels God created is not that important, God did not consider it necessary to tell us.

The study of angels always brings us into a little comparison with man. For one reason we are all God's creations. For the other reason we are completely different from each other. In many ways we are all the same. At least that was God's original intention, but He created man to live on earth as a transitional place: which was a place He could visit with His creation. Eden was perfect, called the Garden of God. It was really Heaven on earth, and man was created with the same glory that angels have now. That's why Adam could commune with God. The Tree of Life now in heaven, was right here in Eden. When man sinned, everything changed. In the next chapter we are going to discuss the Fall of Satan and changes that took place in the universe.

PRAYING TO ANGELS

As powerful as angels are (see chapters 5, 6, and 7) it is unscriptural to pray to them. We Christians can only pray to the Father, in the name of Jesus. Why because all that we have only comes to us through the cross of Christ. Angels cannot answer prayers on their own. They work through the commands and instructions of God the Father. When the Lord Jesus walked the earth, He often spoke about asking His Father: "I will ask My Father to send me twelve legions of angels," but He never told us to pray to angels. (Matthew 26:3) Later He said to ask the Father in the name of Jesus, but never to angels.

There are evil angels out there that will disguise as angels of light pretending to answer and will deceive you. There is a lot of danger in praying to angels, because they do not answer prayers. These angels are disobedient, and no longer serve the Father. The truth is they can't answer prayers. Consequently, any angels posing as having the power to answer prayers should be shunned.

SUMMARY

Often when we meet angels, they appear to us as humans: simple and very humble. A messenger in human terms is the lowest person as far as social status is concerned. When it comes to heaven, messengers I believe are the highest on God's social scale. If you don't believe it, look at who they work for. God trusts them so much He would use the voice of an archangel to announce an important event as the Rapture of the saints.

Here on earth we have all kinds of people on any given social structure. How many from the president of the U.S. down to the common person? Do you realize that there are only two in God's structure: God, and His angels? Then you consider how high angels are. They perform all kinds of tasks. They are healers, (Isaiah.6:6-7); they are intercessory prayer warriors, who pray and get results quickly (Zachariah 1:12). They are miracle workers, (John 5:1-4), who have healed people for ages. Many passages in the Good Book testify that they are God's mighty warriors,

(Daniel 10:13); (2Kings 19:35); (1Chronicles 21:15-16); (Matthew 26:53; John19:36.) That branch of angels is called angelic hosts. You see them everywhere in the bible. The Hosts were there when the Lord was born, and one of them was the one that rolled the stone at the Resurrection. Michael the archangel is one of the stars of the hosts.

Angels are also teachers of apocalyptic literature (Daniel, Zachariah, etc.), they will be preachers of the gospel, the everlasting gospel of Jesus Christ after we are raptured and taken into heaven. As we shall see in Chapter Eight angels are the greatest worshipers in the entire universe. Whatever they do they do it with excellence for the glory of God. They can do everything that God wants done. They were created that way.

CHAPTER 4

Evil Angels

WHO IS SATAN?

S atan is the angel who was called Lucifer. At some point he was one of the angels of God. He was created with special materials including gold. I believe that he was created to look very beautiful. He was also a very highly decorated angel, because of his role as worship leader. I am not sure he was the most beautiful as some say, and that would be naïve because we have not seen the other angels to make that comparison. He was created that way, because he came before large crowds during worship services. His position took him to the very exclusive realms of glory. Being a leader, he joined the ranks of other angels in his class, and very soon he began to see himself in the position of God.

Not only that. Lucifer was also a CHERUBIM, one of the probably higher ranks of the angelic structure. Angels of his type had their own thrones. That meant he had a certain degree of power. That's why other angels rebelled with him. For us humans that meant a lot, and that's why some of us give him more power than he deserves. Be careful, we humans are no match to him or any other angel.

God created all things including Satan, and He does not need anyone to fight Him for what is rightfully His. What the devil is planning to do is nothing short of highway robbery. God created heaven for Himself, and His angels, yet Satan wants the same heaven too. That is really like stealing something that does not belong to him. Satan's personal vendetta against God is totally unfounded, and his plan to usurp God's authority has no basis.

Lucifer was his original name, and it meant morning star. He is no longer the morning star. He may sometimes disguise as the angel of light, because he was created that way, but currently he is the angel of darkness. He wanted God to allow him to remain in heaven so that he could pollute it, but when God kicked him out he declared war. There are many who still believe that Lucifer lives in heaven, but that is simply not true. God allows him to come to heaven from time to time on assignments, but he does not live there. Remember he cannot hide, because God is omnipresent. He is roaming to and from the earth and he rules over the evil angels who fell with him. Satan's plan to usurp God is not how you get anything. That is not how you fight against anyone, especially if you have no matching power. So, he is fighting a losing battle, one he knows he will never win.

Lucifer is also the devil, or the evil one. He is an evil and malevolent spirit. This last name means he is malignant, and all his thoughts are persistently evil. When you are like that you are incapable of good. He knows no love, and he is completely wicked. He does not know how to do anything good. Some have said he is the opposite of God, but that too is a lie. The opposite of good is bad, but the devil is worse than bad. God is not capable of evil, because he created all things. For example, let's say you are a toy maker, if you destroy one of your toys you have not committed evil, because you own the toy. No evil done in destroying one's possession. The devil is evil because he owns nothing and wants to own something that does not belong to him. His whole being is malignant. He does not know anything about goodness. His plan is to take you to the lake of "fire where he is headed." (Revelation 20:10) You won't know this until you are dead. Please don't let him deceive you.

The devil is destined for the lake, so he lies to everyone he meets. That makes him a habitual liar. His chief goal is to deceive people, so he can take them with him. After he got kicked out of heaven he landed on earth, which is not his home. Basically, he is homeless, and a transient, because the earth does not belong to him, and neither is heaven. He is the chief of the occult, the dark world, and witchcraft, and the king of all things evil. Whatever he does may seem good, but his sole aim is to kill you. Most of the people he deceives are young people. He uses your God-given talents to lure you away from God, so that he can lead you away from Christ the Savior. If you die without Christ, the devil will not save you. My advice is to seek Christ when you are young, that way, you are covered by His blood, and you will have a beautiful life in heaven.

As the accuser, he accuses us of how worthless mankind is to God. He does that because he is worthless himself. He lies to us that God either does not exist and will never live up to His word. He believes that everybody is a liar, because he is a liar. In fact, that accusation is the same thing as condemnation. In his mind he believes that we will never amount to anything. That is what he is, because that's what anyone becomes without God. He reminds us of every sin that we have committed, telling us we can never be saved. That's also because he himself can never be saved. He thinks we are all condemned, because he is condemned. Remember that anyone who speaks to you about how bad you are may be telling you about himself. He only succeeds with those who are ignorant of the powerful word of God, and the salvation provided for them by our Lord Jesus Christ.

DEATH

Lucifer was created long before the first man. We know that as a supernatural being, he was wiser and far older than the first humans. Sometimes though, he can make lots of mistakes. For example, the decision to rebel against God is one decision he will regret forever. It has cost him everything. Michael is the head of all angels, higher perhaps than Lucifer, but he never made such mistakes. When God created the first couple He put them in the Garden of Eden. Satan came to them taking the form of a serpent. He used his superior skills to deceive them into thinking that if they ate of the tree of the knowledge of good and evil they would be like God. The first couple fell for his lies and ate of the tree that God had forbidden them from eating. When they ate the tree of the knowledge of good and evil, death came into the world and man has been dying ever since, Gen. 3:6. This is what I call the sting of death. This sting has cost many billions of lives.

Lucifer was created with extraordinary beauty, because he was designed by the God for music, but I don't believe he is the most beautiful, and powerful angel. Michael is the most powerful angel, and I believe that's why he oversees the nation of Israel. Satan had access to the most holy places in heaven to lead the choir in heaven. His beauty was also part of his downfall in that it was the source of his pride. Sooner or later his beauty went to his head and he began to be prideful.

Make no mistake about it, we are no match for the devil. Like most angels he still has power to take human form, take the form of serpents, flies, or anything. He has the power to perform evil signs and wonders. He can even disguise as the angel of light. He has no power over those who have been washed in the blood of our Lord Jesus Christ. He is under our feet.

He is a person who can throw you in a ditch and laugh in your face. Doing evil and seeing people suffer is what pleases him. As far as he is concerned he wants to see every human being spend eternity in hell. Christ our Savior has created a place for you and me. Do not fall into the devil's tricks. Doing good work is not in his nature. That's how far Satan has gone for one who used to be a holy angel. He has no mercy, and his heart is as black as black can be.

After being cast from heaven and knowing that he cannot be redeemed, as you and I are, Satan was seriously hurt. Knowing that a day has been set for his final condemnation the devil is determined to harm the holy ones of God. His main goals are: to steal, to kill and to destroy. He works relentlessly to implement that wicked strategic plan of his. He will go to any length to get it done.

You are here to glorify Christ dear brethren. Whoever you are, no matter how rich and successful you are, always ask yourself if you are doing anything with all your success for God. God sent us into this world to serve Him. That is the purpose for your life, and mine. He did not send us to be a great basketball player, football star, movie star, and whatever you are doing. You've got to find a way to serve God with your skills, your wealth, and your substance. No matter how much success and wealth you have in this world, you have nothing without Christ. All you have will remain here on earth, and you will go out empty. You see that every day. Satan uses wealth to deceive some of us. That's not the chief aim of man. The real aim of man is to serve God who created him. When that happens then he will go out with a bang.

FALL OF SATAN

In the ions of time one of God's own angels who had participated in activities in the most exclusive realms of glory began to contemplate a coup against his Master. While he was still contemplating this wicked coup the LORD God said to him:

> "You have been in Eden, the Garden of God; every precious stone was your covering, the ruby, topaz, and jasper, the sapphire, the turquoise, CHRYSOLITE, onyx, and beryl. The settings and your mountings were made of gold; the pipes were prepared on the day when you were created. You are the anointed cherub that covers, and I made you so. You were upon the holy mountain of God; you walked back and forth between the stones of fire; you were perfect in your ways from the day that you were created, until sin was found in you." By the Multitude of your merchandise they have filled the midst of you with pride and you have sinned; Therefore, I will cast you as a profane out of the Mountain of God; and I will destroy you O covering Cherub from the midst of the stones of fire. Your Heart was lifted up (pride) because of your beauty, you have corrupted your wisdom by reason of your brightness: I will cast you to the ground, I will lay you before kings, that they may see you." (Ezekiel 28:13-19)

There are three statements stating "I will cast you" in the passage. It seemed as if after the LORD God pronounced the last : **"I will cast**

you to the ground," **(Ezekiel 28:17)** a whirlwind swept him up, and he found himself on earth, being mocked and ridiculed by kings of the earth, "is this the man that we have been hearing of, the man who thought he was something, look at him!" Lucifer is the angel who was invited to the meeting with God. You can see he was quite decorated, and he let all these decorations go to his head. **He was made of rubies, topaz, emerald, CHRYSOLITE, onyx, jasper, Sapphire, turquoise, beryl, and gold.** (Ezekiel 28:13)

The high places he had been included: Eden, the Garden of God; the Holy Mountain of God, and the Stones of Fire. That means he could have been one of those angels who covered the Mercy Seat, from where God sat to address the people of Israel. No one could go any closer to the Almighty like the cherubim. To be admitted into all these places was a great privilege for any one. Let us talk about the decorations and qualifications just a little bit.

Lucifer was the most decorated angel, but decorations are not qualifications. They are like badges, golden stars and other golden plates on a military man's uniform. Being where he was as chairman of worship at the throne of the Most- High, he needed to look presentable for the world to see. Let us take the military example. We know that not everyone wears the same attire. As they go higher they acquire more decorations according to the ranks, but they are all just work uniforms.

Qualifications are a little different. We agree they all don't mean very much in the overall scheme of things in God's mind. Let us look at the guy who gets saved. They are baptized and given ministry gifts. Some of us go on to become apostles, prophets, pastors, teachers, and so forth. These titles mean nothing. The important thing is that we have been saved by the grace of God. At the end of the day you are not in heaven because you had the different gifts, and titles. You are there because you have been saved by the grace of God. Lucifer thought all his decorations were qualifications and very soon he began to gloat. His head grew bigger, and bigger and very soon it grew bigger than the level acceptable for his continued existence in heaven. He was cast out.

Judging from his reactions Lucifer did not know that anyone knew about his plan nor did he believe that he did anything wrong. One day the Almighty being who He is had known about it all along. So, he summoned Lucifer to what seemed like a brief work-place conversation saying:

> **"for you have thought in your heart, I will ascend into heaven, I will exalt my throne above the stars of God; I will sit also upon the Mount of the Congregation; in the sides of the north. I will ascend above the heights of the clouds; I will be like the Most-High."** (Isaiah. 14:13-15)

Now that's going too far. Lucifer had kicked himself in the groin.

This is what the angel had planned in his heart so the Mighty One laid it on him. Pretty serious and grievous, don't you think? I could tell the Lucifer did not know that anyone knew about his secret. As the Almighty revealed it to him his eyes grew bigger in his head, as he wandered as if to say: "how did the LORD find out?" Then he remembered that the Almighty is One who knows and sees all things and read minds. Not wise to think that you could hide such plans in the presence of God and get away with them. "Nothing is ever hidden in His sight, but all things are open and laid bare to Him who is Judge of all things." (Hebrews 4:12-13) The real question is how could Lucifer forget that? How could he not know that the Almighty God sees and knows the hearts of those He has created? How could he have lived with the LORD all those billions of years and not understand that the Mighty One is omniscient? That's the problem with sin. Scripture says: "professing to be wise they became fools." (Romans 1:22) Sin always costs us something. During this time the devil did not repent.

Some also think that Lucifer was one of the most powerful angels. If that was true, the section above does not confirm that. He surely lacked wisdom. How could he be powerful and make such mistakes? Again, the answer is in his decorations. God gives all of us certain titles, but at the end of the day the titles do not mean anything. Even I know that when we get to heaven we will all just be His children, and nothing more. That is good enough for me.

I am sure the angel was shocked at what he heard, not because he did not know. He just thought he could get away with it. As he listened he sank in his chair in disbelief. If you notice, the ALMIGHTY One is God, the One from Whom, nothing can be hidden. We must learn that there are no secrets, and no places to hide. At the early stages of the meeting the angel misjudged the magnitude of his sin. He thought the Almighty One was going to give him a warning, and another chance, but sin of this magnitude is unpardonable. Again, Satan had misjudged the situation, and had blundered.

Usually at the point where Lucifer sinned the LORD had given him a lot of chances. Knowing who the devil was, he had convinced himself that it was nothing serious and played it cool. Again, he had seriously miscalculated. As the meeting progressed the ALMIGHTY handed him his sentence when He spoke these words: **"yet thou shalt be brought down to hell, to the sides of the pit."** (Isaiah 14:15) With that remark the devil knew he was done, but it didn't quite reach him until he found himself on earth being mocked by earthly kings. Wait until you see what happened to him when warms filled his body, consuming him alive. I would like you to know that the devil is still crying and regretting the actions he took that led to his demise. I would be too. Knowing who he is he never does. He continued in his rebellion. He was stripped of his power, his position, titles, and whatever reputation he had. At that time the highly decorated angel became the devil, and Satan, and he vowed: "I'll take my revenge on God, and His followers. I will deal with them." I know, and you could tell that those were mere words, because even he knew he was trying to do something that he could never win.

Here's the thing, the LORD God was not surprised that Satan turned out to be what he became at all. **He created Satan, and He decorated him, so the LORD knew, I believe, that the devil was a bad seed right from the beginning.** The Lord Jesus did the same thing. He told His twelve disciples this: "have I not picked you? I know there is the devil among you." The LORD God saw Satan's future, and He knew his end. He knew the devil more than the devil knew himself. That's how He is with us. He knows us more than we know ourselves.

The LORD is the ultimate parent with his children. He knows their attitudes, and He monitors their progress. He knew all along what the devil would be, but He gave him chances. The reasoning here is, when you have power like the ALMIGHTY, you toy with things, and play for time. When the time comes, and the children play the fool you hand them the ropes to hang themselves. The devil was not wise, because he would have known that there was a blazing light all over him, and everyone in heaven. You can't play those kinds of games with God. Just come plain and admit you are wrong and work to change. You and I know pride does not let people like this to repent.

Even to this day some people think the devil was the number two, i.e. next to God, because of his decorations. Nothing could be further from the truth. We know that the bible does not classify him or any one as such. If you look at the text above the Lord said, Lucifer was beautiful, and He created him so. It means the LORD designed him that way. He has the power to that, as King David said:

> "Both riches and honor come of Thee and Thou reigns
> over all; In Thy hand is power and might; in Thy hand
> it is to make great, and to give strength unto all."
> (1Chronicles 29:12)

The truth is Lucifer did not work for those decorations. That is also the difference between the CREATOR, and the creature. The Almighty can do as He pleases to any of us. We must understand that He has all power. He created power. In this case He exercised that power on Lucifer and brought him to his end. He is roaming the earth on a leash like a dog.

The fact is the LORD God knew that there was a devil among His angels, just like the Lord Jesus knew that Judas Iscariot was among His apostles, but He waited for the right time to reveal him. The LORD God made the devil the worship leader, and brought him close, just as the Lord Jesus made Judas to carry and manage the finances of the organization. That is proof of the power of God. He can do anything, and no matter what we think we are nothing to Him.

There's no number two person between the LORD, and anyone of His creations. There is too wide a gap between God and His creations that no one can fill. There is no one like God: (1) He is the Creator; no one else can create; ; (2) He is the Possessor of heaven and earth; He owns everything and everybody; (3) He is the Eternal, and He lives forever; (4) He is Omnipresent, He is omnipresent; (5) He is the Incomprehensible, No one can fully know His ways; (6) He has all knowledge; (7) He is all-seeing; night and day are the same to Him; (8) He is Invincible; He cannot be destroyed; (9) He is El-SHADDAI; He has all power, His power is unlimited; (10) He is all-wise; wisdom belongs to Him; (11) He is the Alpha and Omega, He has no beginning and no end; (12) He is sovereign – He sets the rules upon which the universe operates; (13) He is Infinite, but everything else is finite; (14) He is unknowable, etc. He is too big to be known. Angels have stood before Him since their creation, yet they have not completely known His will. We will study about Him forever. He stands alone apart from all His creation. There's no one like Him. Which one of these attributes do you suppose the devil, or anyone has?

With a word the devil was cast out of Eden, the Garden of God in disgrace to the earth. God caused a fire from within Satan to consume him and made a spectacle of him to a watching crowd of the kings of the world at that time. This happened long, long before Adam. Satan and other angels were created at a time before our own, in eternity past. Satan probably thought the LORD will just forgive him as He has always done, but this was a different day. The LORD treated him as the enemy that he is. Amen.

MICHAEL AND LUCIFER MEET

One day there was war in heaven brought about by the great dragon. Before then the holy angels served God beautifully. As we saw earlier, the devil that was cast from heaven went and regrouped and appeared in heaven to fight to try to take his place. No one apart from God conceived of what Lucifer planned. I think that the devil himself was surprised when he found out that the LORD God knew his thoughts as He read them to him. As he listened, the Lord read him his thoughts, and he knew then that he was in trouble. The Lord knew that something like this was going to happen from the devil's beginning. He knew that Lucifer was a bad seed since creation, and He knew that he would do something like this, but He gave him time, just as the Lord Jesus allow Judas to stay so that He may complete His plan. Though he is the devil, the Lord made him, and He used him for what he was. No one understands the mind of God, and why He allows some of His creatures to do the things they do. The devil was stripped of the glory of God, and some of his powers.

THE POWER OF SATAN

The word of God speaks a lot about Satan, but mainly because of his rebellion against God. That is particularly the reason why he has received so much coverage, but not because he has power. When it comes to comparing him to human beings he is powerful of course, but compared to other angels of his class he is not all that powerful. Most of his followers think of him as powerful, because they compare him to humans. Some people have carried this comparison beyond its limits.

We have seen how decorated he was, but that was also mainly because of his duties as the worship leader in the throne of God. That was one position he held, and it was a high one. It is like you and i. God can make us into anything, like the highest position in government and so on. But when it comes down to it these positions don't change who we are. To add to it he was also an "anointed cherub." (Ezekiel 28.14) That meant he was a covering angel. These were Cherubs or (CHERUBIM) the angels who covered the Mercy Seat in the Arc of the Covenant.

The bible states that he walked to and from the stones of fire, and he was also upon the Holy Mountain of God. This did not mean he had additional powers. The word upon here meant he went to and from the stones of fire, and the Holy Mountain. The Holy Mountain is where God receives worship from His creation. Satan was not God and certainly not a member of the Godhead and did not sit on the Holy Mountain, because he was not being worshiped. I believe He was serving the LORD in those places. I am sure that's where he got carried away.

Some angels have have thrones of their own. These thrones were positions or seats of power, but the bible does not explain how much power these angels had, but they obviously did not have power that came close to the power of the Almighty. The bible does not say that he was the most powerful angel, the wisest or the second in command, or any such thing. We know that he was not the only Cherub. There were four cherubs, including Michael, Gabriel, etc. Michael is the most powerful angel God ever made. That's why he is the prince of all angels, and the Archangel not Lucifer. Michael is an angelic leader in all assignments all over the universe, and that is why he is the angelic host who gets called to watch over the nation of Israel, God's people. The angels who followed Lucifer in his rebellion were not angelic hosts, and we see Michael defeat Satan in (Revelation 12:7-9) as the devil was cast out of heaven.

Satan's plan was to ascend to heaven, raise his throne above the stars of God, sit enthroned in the Mount of Congregation, ascend above the tops of the clouds, and to be like the Most-High. This was his plan, some call this powerful, but it was never achieved. These were empty words. It is one thing to aim at something, and it is another thing to achieve it. Satan was like a little child who had lofty goals which were never achieved, as he was immediately tossed out of heaven along with his supporting cast of angels.

As a supernatural being he is more powerful than humans, but the Lord Jesus came and restored our power against satan. Apart from the Lord, we are powerless before the devil. This time when he came, see the finale of his folly:

"And there was war in heaven: Michael and his angels fought against the dragon; and the dragon and his angels fought and **prevailed not, neither was their place found any more in heaven.** The great dragon was cast out, that old serpent, called the devil and Satan, who deceived the whole world: he was cast out of heaven **and his angels were cast out** with him." (Revelation 12:7-9) Since then Lucifer has embarked on a fight he knows he can't win. That's what happens when you sin you believe lies, even your own lies as your sin takes control of you. Any time you try to fight against God you should know at once that you are outnumbered. His power has no limit. That's how sin came into the world, as the fallen angels went into the world bringing with them their evil.

There's no fight between God and the devil. There are numerous holy angelic beings far superior to Lucifer and his fallen angels. He is no match for the Almighty One. The first time Lucifer was swept away by the word of the Lord, and this time he faced the mighty power of Michael the star of the holy angels, and the archangel.

From above, we can see that there was a time in heaven and earth when evil was never known. All the angels were the holy angels of God until this day when Lucifer and his demons decided to stage this rebellion. In that great discourse above Michael and his angels took it to the devil. In my own words that should remind him of where he has been, to let him know that **he was no more.** God spoke, and His angels took the fight to the **"man of sin,"** and he was vanquished. As he fell, Scripture says a third of the angels in heaven followed him in rebellion. These were no longer holy angels, they became demons, who are responsible for all the evil in the earth today.

DESTINATION OF EVIL ANGELS

There are about two destinations of evil angels, (1) some followed Satan to the earth. These are responsible for all the evil that has existed, and still exists in the earth. (2) The other half of one third is bound up in darkness in chains under the earth awaiting judgment day when they shall be committed to the Lake of Fire prepared for them. (Jude 1:15) On that day all evil angels will be committed into the lake of Fire.

Some believe that Satan was the most powerful angel that God ever created, and that he knew the plans of God. That's false. He was cast out of heaven, God was not about to reward him with the gifts of the Spirit. Nobody knows the plans of God, and we shall see that he did not know anything about the book of revelation.

Maybe he was a powerful archangel, but he was not the only powerful angel. Michael and Gabriel are probably the most powerful. Michael has been the star prince of holy angels since their creation. He is the one that others call to deal with tough situations. That's why he oversees the nation of Israel. That means power. Satan did not even know about the Resurrection of the Lord Jesus. How could he be that powerful without receiving such knowledge? I don't think that people fully understand the difference between the Creator and His creatures. Nobody understands the magnitude of God's power, because He is unknowable. The bible says His power is infinite, His knowledge is infinite, and everything about God is infinite. Every created being is finite.

We also know about the time of the plagues of Egypt. Who do you think was behind the Pharaoh's rebellion against Moses? Of-course it was the devil. During the time of the plagues of Egypt the devil was only able to duplicate three of those plagues. After that he was through, but the LORD was just starting. He brought more and more plagues until He broke Pharaoh's back, and the strongest empire surrendered to Moses. That tells me that Lucifer is no match to the power of God. God allows him to fight, but the devil knows that he is no match. He cannot oppose the Almighty. God gave him some latitude, because He is using him.

SATAN'S PLAN

THIEF

The bible says, "The thief has come but to steal, kill and destroy." (John 10:10) That thief is Satan. He has stolen a lot of things from us. The first thing he stole was the earth which belongs to us. As soon as he was dropped here he made it his. The earth was made for man, so it became his as he tricked the first couple. The other thing he stole from us was our relationships. He has destroyed marriages, and other relationships. Once relationships fail we are plunged in depression, and he robs us of the companionship that we once had with our spouses. He causes sibling rivalries, and brings siblings into war against each other, and thereby stealing the families.

He steals our wealth by leading us into wrong investments, which will ultimately fail, and he will plunge us into poverty. He can also rob us of true treasures, by causing us not to trust God. One of the simplest tricks he has is to lie to us that there's no God. Majority of the world has been deceived this way. He is the reason for the unbelief that permeates the whole world today. For those already in his grip they do not fill his pinch, except those of us who are saved. He has lured many of our young men and women into drugs, alcoholism, fame and sudden death. The devil was a thief in the Garden of Light, and after a while he forgot that he could be caught. That ultimately led to his death.

KILLER

He does not care about you or me, and even about himself. He knows that he is doomed, and he has vowed to kill every single one of us. He is responsible for all the killings in the world. Somebody who does not care about himself cannot care about anything or anyone else. He is a lonely person, has no friends, and family. He is not your brother, friend, or relative.

He does not know anything about love. If he gives you something, he is doing it for one purpose, and one purpose only, to kill you. He makes some people rich, and famous, only because he wants to kill them. He does not need money, and he does not need titles, and so he gives them to those who crave these things. That way they can trust him, and he will take you with him to hell.

He does not know anything about relationships, because he has no relationships. Everything around him is doomed to destruction. He knows nothing about love, care, and compassion. He knows about erotic love, which belittles women, or men, and leads them to sadistic murders of those involved. Love is not in his nature. He cannot help anyone, and everything he does is to achieve his deadly mission. He does not believe in good, or love. As a spirit he has no heart, feelings, love, care, and compassion. No matter how much he pretends to love, his goal is to kill you. Satan is a killer in a place where the eyes of the LORD are watching. Eventually he forgets that the corpses of the people he has killed are lying all around being found by those who are watching. Before long, his own tricks will reveal who the killer is.

DESTROYER

He is a destroyer. Satan has seen the best in heaven, and after he was driven from all that indescribable beauty he can't stand anything that carries any kind of beauty. His mission is to destroy. Thank

God that He is not like us that have no power. He could not let a horrible thing like Satan destroy His beauty. Left in charge Satan will lead everything to destruction. Do you see the devastation caused by storms, Islamic suicide bombings causing carnage upon carnage? That's what Satan likes. Do you see the millions killed in auto accidents every year, the millions of people destroyed by drunk driving every year, and those killed by plane crashes every year? He revels in these sorts of things. Destruction, murders, and bloodshed are his party. Thank God for being our God for loving us. He sent His Son to save us, and to prepare us against this evil of a monstrosity, Satan.

Somebody who is a destroyer cannot build anything. He is not one who can build a business, a government, a city, or a society. Where these structures are built he helps to tear down, and where they are being built he will help with the destruction. Why? Because he knows no love, and because love is what holds things together, and it builds. Pretty soon he forgets that he has over done it, and that ultimately leads to his own destruction.

THE ANSWER

Satan caused so much pain before Christ came to the extent that the heavens and people rejoiced when Christ was born. After He was born Satan got Him nailed to the cross thinking, I have got Him now, but little did he know that the cross was exactly Satan's elimination. The Cross was God's answer for the sting of death placed on man by the devil. As the Lord triumphed at the cross Satan was defeated because the salvation of followers was secured. This meant that men would not die that second death. The Lord left us with two weapons to fight the evil one: (1) His word: "the weapons of our warfare are not carnal, but mighty through God, to the demolishing of strongholds, destroying arguments and every pretension that sets itself up against the knowledge of God, and taking captive every thought to the obedience of Christ." (2 Corinthians 10:4-5)

(2) The Lord's name: Being exalted the Scripture says of the Lord

Jesus, "at the Name of Jesus every knee should bow, in heaven, and on earth, and under the earth, and every tongue confess that Jesus Christ is Lord to the glory of God the Father." (Philippians 2:10-11) For us humans, armed with these tools Satan was defeated forever. Holy angels are made to fight demons for us. They are deployed everywhere to beat the devil at his game. They know his every move. The Lord is way ahead of his every plan, but they cannot fight without our action. We can't just sit there. Our job is easy: Scripture says, "believe on the Lord Jesus, and your family, and friends shall be saved, and you shall have freedom provided by Christ, and His Cross."

SATAN JUDGED

"And I saw an angel coming down out of heaven having the key to the bottomless pit and holding in his hand a great chain. He seized the dragon named the devil, or Satan, and bound him for a thousand years. He threw him into the Abyss, and locked and sealed the Abyss to keep him from deceiving the nations anymore until the thousands are ended." (Revelation 20:1-3)

Friends, Satan and his demons think they are great, but the passage above says otherwise. It says they are living on borrowed time. One day they are roaming free, but the next day they are snatched and confined. His life is that of a runaway prisoner. Don't let him deceive you. They have no place to take you. This passage tells us that for a thousand years Satan will be captured and detained for a short period. It also tells us the process of his judgment and banishment has just begun. First, he is taken to the Abyss, a place darker than darkness where he will live for one thousand years. He is released to give him a chance to deceive more people and give people a chance to choose the cross of Jesus Christ. Note that God is using him to do His work, but he thinks he is powerful. Watch what happens later.

At an undetermined time, "he is snatched and thrown into the lake burning with sulfur, where the beast and the false prophet are. They will be tormented day and night for ever and ever." (Revelation 20:10) There's a literal lake of fire waiting for Satan and his angels. His condemnation starts right after the tribulation period.

GOD'S WORLD

Out of heaven, Satan was not as free as he thought he would be. Nobody escapes the watchful eyes of the Almighty. He knew that, but he still tried to deceive people. According to Job Chapter One, Satan finds out that he is not at liberty to destroy everything, but he can only touch those things which God has allowed him to. Of-course we know that, because he senses the presence and power of God everywhere he goes.

What that means is that the earth is not his. God created the world for man not for Satan. What he has is really what we have given him, and his life is really in the Mighty hand of God. Many are deceived to believe that he has comparative power against God. Nothing could be further from the truth. The truth is Satan has put himself in a game against the Almighty who created him, and everywhere he goes he is always fulfilling the purposes of the Mighty Jesus Christ. Ultimately the earth belongs to God, and if we humans wise up and follow Christ then we could deal with the devil as we should, and God will be vindicated.

"The word of God is forever settled in heaven," Ps.119:89. That means when God speaks, it is done. No force or power can prevent God's word from performing what He has intended. His word has keeping or staying power.

COULD SATAN CREATE HIS OWN UNIVERSE?

This is a question that has never been asked before. I thought instead of the devil going about accusing God, holy angels, and the people of God, why didn't he just create his own universe? That would have been a sensible thing to do. Laying aside all the attributes of God, let us examine the man of sin and see how he stacks up against with these inabilities: wisdom, power, creative ability giving life, lack of love, and destroyer.

LACK OF WISDOM

When it comes to wisdom we have already discussed the wisdom of God and those include the attributes of God. We know that the devil outmatches any of us. God alone is omnipresent, omnipotent, All-seeing. God alone is holy, omniscient, perfect, and sovereign, etc. The devil does not have the wisdom of God. He is not omniscient, not perfect, or any of these attributes. Everything about God has to do with power.

We saw the situation in Egypt. The devil was able to duplicate only the first three plagues. After that he was done, but the LORD was just starting. In the end the Egyptians who did not want to release Israel, began to force them out. They gave them clothes, gold, and other things to go and celebrate the same God they have been opposing.

LACK OF POWER

One of the attributes of God is His power. That means any kind of power. Scripture says His power is infinite. Nobody else has that kind of power. Every creature has a measure of power, but no one has the power like the LORD has. He has the power to do all things, see all things, know all things, create, sustain all things; the list goes on and on. Everything about the LORD is a wonder. I just can't wait to meet Him in the future. People wonder, what are we going to do in Heaven? I believe there will be much for us to do. The angels are studying about His will. We write books about important personalities, but when it comes to God we could write a billion books, and not come close to exhausting the subject of God.

CREATIVE INABILITY

Satan has no ability to create. Creation is the ability to bring things into existence. It is not just originating things, but also the ability to give life. Those two abilities go together. You can't just create things you have to be able to give life. When God created everything, without angels and humans the world was still teaming with life. The trees and the animals had life and that's what made things beautiful. If you just create things with no life things won't be interesting.

Satan has never created anything, and he cannot give life. His personality is such that he cannot create, because he cannot love, and he is a destroyer. To create anything, you cannot be a destroyer. Added to that is the fact that He cannot sustain anything. Sustaining is like creation. Therefore, Satan's destructive ability takes away his ability to create and to sustain. He is by nature not a creator.

LACK OF LOVE

The LORD God gave us love as the glue that holds all things together. Without it everything falls apart. Marriages are held together by the love of God and without it, things become chaotic. Animals are held together in their unions the same way in their unions. Some of them are completely dominant, but they understand that they need each other. They are held together by the power of God. With us humans I know that without love there's no holding power.

In the so-called civilized societies, the glue that holds together has worn thin. God sent His Son to die for us, because He loved us so much. As the famous verse says, "for God so loved the world that He gave His only Begotten Son, that whosoever believes in Him should not perish, but have everlasting life." (John 3:16) The key words here are "so loved the world; believes in Him, will not perish, but have everlasting life." You see, He does not just love us, but He has given us His love that holds us together. We are talking about the devil here. He cannot suddenly change from his malignancy to a decent individual. He does not have the properties needed to create.

A DESTROYER

The devil is a destroyer, one who destroys anything around him. That stands in the way of any plans he had to create anything. A destroyer cannot be a builder. Those two qualities are mutually exclusive. God alone is a builder, because He has the wisdom, power, and love. It is important to note that without God man becomes exactly like the devil. He tends to destroy everything including himself. He has invented automobiles, airplanes, and other types of engines, but everything we make brings destruction. How many people get killed by automobile accidents and airplanes every year?

To be a builder you must have love. Satan is persistent in evil, and every fiber of his being is evil. God is however persistent in love. When you are as godless as the devil is everything leads to destruction. He is not learning to become evil he is already malignant. He cannot be saved, because he is beyond saving. A destroyer cannot be a builder, and neither can he be a creator.

THE OPPORTUNITY

Since he fell Satan has had his opportunity to create his own universe where he can make his own rules and roam wild without control. The life he wanted seems logical to me that he could easily get it by creating his own universe. As we look around we see nothing of the kind.

He has the chance to achieve his dreams. Even if he were given this universe he would eventually destroy it, because that is who he is. Therefore, the plan of our God will go on until the consummation, as He said. He has given Satan all the time he needed. The devil knew that the gap was just too wide. Setting aside the attributes of God, the devil does not have what it takes to create. Lucifer has no wisdom, power, creativity, love, sustainability or keeping power, and a multitude of other attributes which God has. Satan does not have what it takes to create. Blessed be JEHOVAH, our God forever. Amen.

CHAPTER 5

Angelic Superiority

ANGELIC SUPERIORITY

Any time you think about angels, at some point you wind up comparing them to humans. Some people seem to imply that somehow man is God's highest creation. We humans are seated in heavenly places in Christ, but that is not because we were worthy or have earned it. We are seated with Christ because He came and redeemed us, not because of anything we have done. From the beginning the Psalmist said:

> "When I consider your heavens, the work of your fingers, the moon and stars, which you have set in place, what is the man that you are mindful of, the son of man that you care for? You have made him a little lower than the heavenly beings and crowned him with glory, and honor. You have him rule over the works of your hands; you put everything under his feet: all flocks and herds and the beasts of the field, the birds of the air, and the fish of the sea, all that swim the parts of the sea." (Psalm 8:3-8)

This passage considers all that God has made and says that man is made lower than the heavenly beings. It says man was created a little lower than the angels. What does it mean by little? After considering all the the facts it seems the way is lot lower than they. The object of this chapter is to show you how higher angels are compared to man.

Men and angels are creatures of the Most-High God. We are like siblings: one flesh, and the other spirit, but we are miles apart from each other in many ways. In considering the question we are going to be looking at the following: environment, Nature, Clothed with Glory, Knowledge and Wisdom, Spirit, Strength, Unlimited Access, Holiness, and absence of Uncertainty.

ENVIRONMENT

One of the reasons for angelic superiority is because they live in heaven. The Lord made His angels to live with Him in heaven where there is life, but man was made to live on earth where there is little or no life. Remember when the LORD created the earth it was full of glory, but king David who asked the question was living at a time when the earth had changed. At his time man had sinned and the world was no longer in its original state.

When angel Gabriel came to Zachariah he said, "I am Gabriel that stand before God." What is standing before God? One thing about being before God is you enjoy life and you experience joy, because, "In His presence there is the fullness of joy and I don't know if angels eat or not, but they are in a perpetual state of joy that is characteristic of life in heaven. That tells us that they experience real life. In His presence there is also peace. This is a peace that flows like rivers of water; a peace that is above human understanding, because He is the Prince or Author of peace. It is a place where there is actual rest. In our world of turmoil what we really need is peace. John the Revelator expressed the fact that things were so loud in heaven. That tells me another thing: that speaks of happiness. When people are happy they shout. Being in heaven also means liberty, because the Spirit of God is there. That comes with the dancing and screaming. Nobody sits quietly when they are happy. The presence of God brings joy, peace, happiness and freedom.

NATURE

If you noticed, angels are created like God Himself. He is spirit, and they too are spirit. (Hebrew 1:7) For every creature that God created He marked them with His image, except perhaps animals. Much has been discussed about the spiritual nature and more will be discussed later. A spirit being is one of the most fascinating things that God created. The bible speaks of the living creatures which have different features. I have the impression that we will see very strange spiritual beings in heaven.

The fact that a person can exist with nothing but air, is quite hard for us humans, and we can never quite understand it. How does a spirit exist with all the violent storms blowing around? That says a lot about the genius and power of God. Without a body that means they can live in the sky, under the earth, under water, and anywhere. They really do not need houses to live in and do not change clothes. There is nothing to wear clothes on. Spiritual beings do not get sick. No diseases can infect them. They do not experience pain and they do not get tired. They live in heaven where there is no death, and so they live forever. They can go through rocks, fences, water, and they can survive any type of atmospheric environment. In many ways, they are a species that have very low or no maintenance.

We exercise because we want to lose weight, and to be strong, but there are supernatural beings that do not need exercise. In other words, they are always healthy, and amazingly strong. No wonder the scripture says, "they excel in strength." If you think about it, spirit beings have nothing but power and energy.

Their life is perfect or complete. Heaven is also a place where there is no uncertainty. There's never going to be a time when something is going to go wrong. No. God's power guarantees that. On earth you may have a good time today, but tomorrow is a different day. I mean you may have the best life today and die tomorrow. You may die of natural disasters, deadly diseases, and all kinds of situations that cause us all kinds of problems. That's why many people do not even believe that there is a place like heaven. They only imagine it. We know it is there for those who put their faith in the Lord Jesus Christ. Heaven is a place where you have your best day everyday of your life, and that never ends.

CLOTHED WITH GLORY

We have touched on the glory a little bit earlier. When you encounter some angels in their original state chances are they are going to have a shiny or sparkling covering around him. That is called the glory of God. Holy angels are clothed with the glory of God, which is the same glory that God has. This aura or covering produces a permanent glow.

The glory of God is an anointing from God that gives them power. It also gives them wisdom, understanding, and any kind of power that God wants them to have. We see that in the Transfiguration Episode of our Lord Jesus, as He revealed His Original glory to His disciples at Mount Transfiguration. In that incident His face, and clothing turned into a bright light like the sun. The disciples fell, facedown terrified as they saw the glory of their Lord. They could not stand its brightness, and power.

The glory of God is powerful. We human beings are sinful because of our flesh. The first man was created with that same glory, but when he sinned he lost the glory. The same thing happened to evil angels. They lost their glory because the rebelled against God. Not only did they lose their glory, but they have lost some of their power also. Holy angels continue to have their glory.

The glory of God makes it possible for angels to live in heaven in the presence of God. Without that anointing angels will seize to be holy, and perfect, and cannot come before God. The glory of God is a symbol or purity, of righteousness, and holiness. God is holy, and powerful, and without glory no one can approach the LORD. That's why humans cannot approach angels. When Adam lost the glory, he lost the ability to have communion with His maker. It is not possible for everyone to approach heavenly bodies unless they have accepted Christ. That's why when you pass on into the next life the Lord will give you a body that will take you to heaven. The bible also says that when we, the redeemed of the Lord, die we are instantly transformed into a new body to enable us to stand before God. Everyone cannot stand before God. So, the only way to go to heaven is to be saved and cleansed by the blood of the Lord Jesus Christ to enable you to have that glorified body. The unsaved cannot go to heaven. They don't have the garments required to grant them access into heaven. The Lord is the only One who qualifies us by His blood, and power.

Therefore, the idea that everybody goes to heaven after they die is false. Heaven is not for dead people who have not received Christ. It is for the redeemed of the Lord. Don't leave earth without it. Angels are superior because they live in heaven where we are striving to go, and they have eternal life, and they don't need to be saved. They are already holy.

KNOWLEDGE AND WISDOM

Scripture says, "Wisdom comes from the LORD: wisdom and understanding come from His mouth." (Proverbs 2:6) Angels spend their lives in the presence of God. That gives them the chance to learn God's ways and acquire His wisdom. Studying in our universities does not come from God, and therefore, it is not wisdom. Wisdom is the word of wisdom from God. It comes by revelation by the Holy Spirit. When the Lord Jesus was on earth He told many parables. People could not get enough of them. His presence was like a magnet, because those who came did not want to leave. And so, it is with the presence of God. His words were the word of God and they were full of wisdom. His words were like hidden treasures that people could harvest.

Angels are superior, because they have divine knowledge and wisdom. That's why they knew about the Advent of Christ, and the Resurrection before it happened. Heaven is the source of information, so they receive it as soon as it is available. Scripture says they know everything on the earth. They know all things in the skies above, the earth, under the earth, and all living things that God has created.

Angels also have perfect knowledge, which means they have complete knowledge, lacking nothing. They have full knowledge about heaven and earth, and the universe. It's one thing to know something, but it is another thing to be able to retain or remember it. Angles have perfect knowledge, and when they learn something they retain it. We humans simply don't have that kind of power.

STRENGTH

Angels are superior because they excel in strength. (Psalm 103:20) At the appearance of angels any natural thing seems to lose power all by itself. Iron gates no matter how firm they might be always just fall apart by the appearance of an angel. Our machine guns and any weapon systems made by man become useless when faced by angelic appearance. Don't think that we can go to war with angels. That is not possible, because their power is superior to anything we have. We will prove that as we study the persecutions that the early church faced after angels came to their aid.

We can liken an angel to somebody who has been exercising all their life when it comes to their strength. They have unbelievable amounts of energy. They praise God seven days per week, every week, and every month, forever and that's why scripture says, "bless the LORD ye His angels who excel in strength. (Psalm 103:20) They are full of energy. They never rest. They praise God seven days a week, every week, and forever and ever. They are also like young men of about fifteen through seventeen, frozen in their youth forever. Imagine how much energy they may have. Endless amounts of energy. They feel on top of the world all the time. They can tear down mountains and conquer anything, anyone in the universe. They can run thousands of miles without rest. They have boundless energy. They are like machines that never break down. We see accidents happen every day. Buildings burn down, but helpless babies emerge from the rubble untouched. How do you explain that? Angels can conduct rescue missions that man can never do.

UNLIMITED ACCESS

Angels have unlimited access to any place in the universe. They are in the air, under the sea, under the earth, and in the fire, where no human being can go. Unlimited access means unrestricted entry into any place in the universe. What I am saying is that God sends His angels all over the universe, so they are made to penetrate these areas with ease. These places would be impossible for humans.

During the Resurrection of the Lord we were told Mary Magdalene went to the tomb to anoint the Holy Body, but what did she find? The disciples themselves were so afraid of the tomb they were not there when the Lord rose. Heaven had angels as witnesses to this great event. They are fearless, and death can do them no harm, because they are holy.

At its beginning, the Church was presented with all kinds of problems. Peter was locked up in prison at least two times. The angels of the Lord were able to go into the prisons to let the apostles out. The apostles received the help they needed with the angelic involvement. Just when the back of the church was against the wall angels showed up. That kept the Church on its feet, sending a message that the church is not an earthly institution. The lesson here is that angels have unlimited access anywhere in the universe. They can go anywhere, live anywhere, defeat any enemy with ease. They are a special force equipped with power to deal with any situation in the entire universe. (Psalm 103:20)

HOLINESS

Angels are also superior because they are holy. Our Lord acknowledged their holiness at least three times in the Bible. Let me remind you that only God **alone is holy**, but He shares His holiness with those close to him. As a result, angels are defined as being holy by the Lord Himself. Therefore, they are righteous, and perfect.

Righteousness is the ability to do the right thing at the right time and all the time. Angels are holy, because they are righteous. This is what makes them unapproachable by humans. Angels are holy, because God is holy, and they are empowered by the Holy Spirit.

They are perfect in everything they do. That means complete. They can do everything right all the time. They do not make mistakes. Perfection has to do with not having defects, being flawless, imbued with absolute excellence. Angels do not have to go to school. Everything they want to know is given by the Holy Spirit. That's because they have intuitive knowledge. The Spirit of God gives that kind of knowledge. When the Lord walked the earth, His angels were not seen but they were there. They heard everything He taught the disciples. After he rose from the dead they knew everything He taught the disciples. That's why they reminded the disciples, "He has risen as He said." You get the impression here that angels have superior intelligence. Their minds are fresh, and alert, absorbing the word of the Lord.

Holiness is what radiates the glow around angels and that is also powerful. That's what makes them unapproachable. Anything sinful cannot come close to angels, because they are holy. Nothing natural can come close to them. Their Holiness absorbs or burns up anything sinful. It's like when a light runs into darkness, it consumes it. That's why the prison gates gave way, and everything does the same at the appearance of angels. Don't be fooled by those who say angels are friends, and brothers. I mean they cannot have close friendships like us humans. They have a divine element in them, which makes them very powerful. Unless they let us, it is practically impossible to go near them. They come close sometimes when sent by God.

ABSENCE OF UNCERTAINTY

Superiority also has to do with where you live. Surely heaven where angels live is far superior to where you and I live. Some think they can approach angels anytime they feel like. That's not true. Angels are spirits and they live in the spiritual part of the universe called heaven. That means that they have a lifestyle that is far superior to ours. They cannot live on earth, because that is not where they were designed to live. Heaven is a place where there's no uncertainty. That means there are no surprises. In heaven the power of God assures that there are no incidences. There have never been, there are none now, and there will never be any.

For example, there are no accidents. There are no natural disasters and they will never be any. No hurricanes that are going come around and destroy houses, cause damages costing millions of dollars, etc. No unforeseen situations. God is the Alpha and the Omega, who is the beginning and the end. In other words, He brings in a future free of problems. There is no sickness of any kind. There are no diseases, and no viruses. Problems are solved billions of years in advance. All you have is what the bible calls fullness of joy, and everlasting bliss. It's totally indescribable. Heaven is what we call life. In the next chapter we shall discuss another dimension of angelic superiority called the POWER OF ANGELS.

CHAPTER 6

The Power of Angels

WHAT IS POWER?

P ower is the exertion of abundant energy, the ability for someone to impose his will or influence on others. Simply put, power is the possession of strength. Scripture says:

"Praise the LORD you His angels who Excel in strength."
(Psalm 103:20)

There are many dimensions of power, and we will be discussing many of them in this chapter. Scripture says as quoted above, angels excel in strength. That means they have more power than any other spiritual beings in the universe. Who might the bible be comparing them to? They are compared to humans, fallen angels, and perhaps wild beasts. That statement shows that they have been tested in battle. Remember that these creatures were not made yesterday. They have been around for billions of years. They have proven their strength. They have been tested, and they are mighty in battle. We also know that their source is the Almighty Himself who has infinite resources of power.

SPIRIT BEINGS

I believe that the first creations of God were spiritual beings, called angels. He created them like Himself as spirits. (Hebrews 1:7) As we saw in chapter 3 angels are incorporeal, they are not made of have flesh and blood like humans. When you think about it, a spirit is synonymous with power. It is someone who by nature has massive amounts of energy and strength. They are designed to have strength by God. Angels are almost the way God is, and that is power. Scripture describes God as the Almighty, the One mighty in battle, the LORD of hosts, and whose power is infinite. God fills the universe in His omnipresence and He gives strength to His angels, because He is power.

FROZEN IN TIME

Angels are like young people of the ages of sixteen through eighteen years old frozen in time forever. These are the ages where young people think they are invincible. At these ages people can do and conquer anything they come up against. They have a lot of energy, and a lot of strength. I had the opportunity to watch my friend's young boy and girls who came to move my things from my house. I watched them pick up the big couches as if they were picking up dry leaves. They worked all day, but it seemed as if they were just starting. They were dripping with sweat, but even that made them work harder. At the end they just picked their things and left. They had been working all day without rest, and they looked as fresh as they would have continued working for many more hours.

Angels are the same as these young people. I am talking about the energy levels and strength of angels. They have huge energy levels and power. Their power is above that of our machines no matter how big, and powerful our machines may be. Human machines will break down, but angels never get tired. The psalmist said angels are ministers of God created as a flame of fire. (Psalm.104:4) That verse of scripture I believe is describing the energy and activity levels of angels. They worship God seven days per week, thirty days a month, twelve months per year, and forever and ever. Nobody expects humans to have such strength, but it is interesting to know that there are living creatures that can. That is a testimony of the genius of our God.

PRINCIPALITIES AND POWERS

Principalities and powers are a New Testament term which describes different angelic powers and rankings, good or bad. Most of us think that this term refers only to evil powers. No, there are Holy principalities and powers too. These powers are located above the earth, these are God and His holy angels in heaven. They consist of holy angels in the highest heaven. God and His angels occupy the highest heaven, and Satan and his demons occupy the second heaven. The definition of power is the ability to influence others, so the kingdom of God rules over the second heaven, the earth, and the entire universe. Satan and his demons, rule over the earth. Therefore, the higher principality rules over the lower principality. It follows therefore, that God and His angels rule over or have more power over evil principalities, the evil angelic powers rule over humans. We can't just match their power. We just can't match their power.

(Ephesians 1:21; Colossians 2:10)

You do not have to go too far to see the two highest powers at work. We Christians are servants of God, and therefore, we belong to the highest principality. I am sure you are aware of the violence, murders, auto accidents, and the drunkenness that are rampant in our cities. This is Satan's philosophy of life. Most people in this country and all over the world serve Satan. His philosophies have permeated our political, social, and economic lives throughout the world. Scripture warns us Christians to:

"Put on the whole armor of God that ye may be able to stand against the wiles of the devil. We wrestle not against flesh and blood, but against evil principalities, against powers and the rulers of the darkness of this world against spiritual wickedness in heavenly places." (Ephesians 6:10-18)

Scripture is our guide, and it tells us that there are these evil spiritual Principalities and powers that are higher than us, (we cannot see them) and they are more powerful than we are. It says there is a war going on in the heavens, and it says the war is not against your human brother or sister, but against these spiritual powers of Satan and his angels warring against us. As Christians, we must put on the whole armor of God, so we can be protected by God against Satan's forces. With the armor we are safe and protected by the love of the highest spiritual Power who is God and His holy angels. These are the wars that holy angelic hosts are engaged in against the powers of darkness.

ANGELIC THRONES

Scripture states that Jesus Christ created all thrones: visible and invisible. (Colossians 1:16) The word throne means a seat of authority. Just as we have certain levels of power here on earth, in the spiritual realms they have certain levels of power. Thrones may be for spiritual beings or services, for example, the throne of God, and the throne of grace. Thrones were created for the Lord Himself, but it seems after Satan rebelled the thrones by some of evil angels became evil thrones. I am not saying that the Lord created evil thrones. No.

I believe thrones are for spiritual beings who have gained certain rankings within a spiritual system. Everybody does not have a throne. They are for a ruling class of that spiritual system. I believe that high angels like Michael, and Gabriel have their own thrones. Even the twelve elders at the throne of God have their own thrones. These angels have power over the angels they supervise. For example, Michael is the archangel, so he supervises all angels, and angelic hosts. Gabriel may be overseeing all messengers.

POWER IN HOLINESS

We have used the holiness of angels quite a bit in this book, but that is because it is an important term. Holiness is not just a process of sanctification or setting apart saints for the purposes of God, it is a power of God. Holiness is a part of God's purity. It is what glows in angels, able to shatter everything evil. That's why we cannot come into the presence of God unless we have something that protects us. That's also why Adam could communicate with God after he sinned.

Holiness has a shattering effect on anybody, or anything evil. The holiness of angels is not their own, it is from God. It destroys other beings, spiritual and visible. That's why holy angels are very deadly toward other beings, including humans. (Daniel 10:21) Humans cannot in any way or form come into the presence of holy angels. We are like evil in their presence and that often spells disaster.

POWER OVER HUMANS

Holy angels live in the highest heavens, so they have power over those who inhabit the lower heavens: that is the second and third heavens. As a result, we cannot interact with these beings as we do our human friends. Below is passage that shows why we can't:

> "And, behold a hand touched me, which set me
> upon my knees and upon the palms of my hands.
> And he said unto me, O Daniel a man
> greatly beloved, understand the words that I
> speak unto thee, and stand upright: for unto
> thee I am **now sent.** And when he had spoken
> this word unto me I stood trembling." (Daniel 10:10-11)

This angel is Gabriel, a powerful angel who was sent to the prophet Daniel. He tried to speak to the prophet yet for fear of him Daniel was trembling like a leaf. Just his appearance overwhelmed Daniel. The prophet had no strength to come before Gabriel. That tells me that angelic beings are more powerful than humans or any of our physical objects. Our weapons such as iron gates, machine guns, and computers are completely powerless before them.

Before coming to Daniel this angel came against the enemy power of demons in the land of Persia. He had to summon Michael for help. The fact that he came to Daniel means that he had partly defeated those demons. We are talking about probably millions of demons against one holy angel. The battle was not done yet. He barely made it through to bring Daniel the answer to his prayers. Then he took with him Michael, this ferocious warrior. This is one of the examples given in the bible that speaks of the work of holy angels. We tend to think that angels have nothing to do. No, they have work that we humans cannot do. They were created for this very reason to take care of the enemies of God.

POWER OVER OTHER BEINGS

Holy angels have power over other spiritual beings. It takes very few holy angels to defeat evil angels. Scripture reports t: "there was war in heaven. Michael and his holy angels fought with the dragon and his angels. The dragon and his followers did not prevail, nor was there a place found for the dragon and his angels in heaven any longer." The passage above just puts it mildly. It was a ferocious war between the forces of good and evil. Satan turned heaven into a war zone. You know what happens when enemies meet. It can be very deadly, and that's what it was. He was met by the archangel Michael, the prince of all angels of God. Finally, Satan and his followers were cast out once again. This time it was for good and has forever been subjected to angels of his rank. Satan is still being used by God for His purposes. (Revelation.12:7-9)

On Resurrection Day the angels were the first on the scene. The disciples did not believe in that Resurrection, even though He had told them He will rise again. Praise God He did not leave things to chance. He sent His angels to be eye-witnesses. The disciples brought spices that morning even after He was risen. They were greeted with the good news of the Resurrection. There were many angels when you consider the accounts of the other Gospels. The angel from Matthew's gospel is the one we are focusing on. His power is shown in rolling a large boulder that could have taken a whole city to roll. His fierce countenance caused a lot of fear among the apostles. People had never seen anyone like him. He was like a monster and even the keepers of the tombs collapsed because of his scary appearance. No one could stand the site of that angel. It was the first time that people had had such a scary experience of an angel of God. If you met such a man somewhere, what would you do? In their original appearances it is impossible for humans to approach them.

The reasoning behind this angel is to show how strong angels can be, and we are going to discuss more in the next chapter. The important thing is that angels were the first witnesses of the resurrection and whatever people think on earth, the Resurrection was recorded in the archives of heaven.

ANGELIC FIGHTERS

The title here denotes the confirmation that angels are not the weak beings that you and I have always known them to be. They are the fiercest fighters on the face of the universe. When asked by the Sanhedrin: are you a King? The Lord replied:

> "My kingdom is not of this world: if my kingdom were of this
> World, then would My servants fight that I should not be
> Delivered to the Jews: but now is my kingdom not from
> Hence." (JOHN 18:36)

Who was the Lord referring to in that response? He was referring to His servants: angelic hosts, God's fighters. They are not like any fighters we have seen, but they are the fiercest military on the face of the universe. Their mission remains peaceful though, but they are equipped with weapons and tools that are totally unconventional.

MIRACLE POWER

Angels also have the power to do miracles. In John chapter 5 an angel went into the pool once every year to stir the water. After the water was stirred whoever got into the pool first was healed of any condition he or she had. The angel who went into the pool to stir the water is unnamed.

They also have power to punish with disease or even death. Gabriel punished the Priest Zacharias with dumbness for his lack of faith. The priest failed to believe when the angel told him that his wife would have a son. He went against the word of God. Gabriel even told him that he stands before God. That was all he needed to believe. When he doubted he was hit with dumbness, until the miracle came through. (Luke 1:20) We know that angels cannot perform miracles on their own. All they can do is be in accordance with God's will. Usually they are sent by God to do anything He wants them to do.

POWER THROUGH DREAMS

Dreams might be spooky, but they are a source of power in angelic realms. There are a lot of verses concerning dreams in the Bible, and God uses dreams to communicate with His people. When you have a dream, you are in the spirit. They are not a natural thing. Being in the spirit is ideal for God, then He can speak spirit-to-spirit and you can receive and understand better. God uses dreams to send His angels to provide help to humans or solve problems. When the Lord Jesus was born, and Herod wanted to kill Baby King Jesus, the angel of the LORD came to Joseph in a dream saying:

> "arise and take the young child and his mother and flee
> To Egypt, and be there until I bring you word for Herod
> will seek the young child to destroy Him." (Matthew.2:13)

The next day Joseph did as he was told. After the days were over the angel of the Lord appeared to Joseph in Egypt in a dream saying:

> "arise and take the young child and the mother and go
> into the land of Israel for they are dead which
> sought the young child's life." (Matthew 2:20)

Dreams are one way that God uses to send angels to people that He is working with. What we saw there was an effort to spare Baby Jesus' life. While Herod wanted to kill the baby Jesus, God used dreams to send

His angel to speak to Joseph so as to save the child's life. Angels have the power to do all sorts of things. Dreams can be deadly, that's why people die in their sleep. Be careful not to sin against God or He will send His angels to take you out.

CHAPTER 7

God's Mighty Warriors

MIGHTY WARRIORS

The bible declares: "Bless the LORD ye His hosts who do His pleasure..." (Psalm 103:21) When you read anything about the LORD of hosts, that refers to the Commander of angelic hosts. You'll never see angels dressed in military uniforms, yet He never goes anywhere without them. Not because He is afraid, not because He needs protection, but because He is the King of the universe. He is not like other kings. He is a King whose power is infinite. He is the greatest King, and a king needs His servants to serve Him.

This chapter is about angelic hosts. When John the Revelator saw one of them he said: "Then I saw another mighty angel coming from heaven... (Revelation 10:1) The only word the apostle could find when he saw this angel was the word mighty angel. What did he mean? We will be discussing their might and strength when we look at God's mighty angels below.

Most bible readers do not really pay attention to angelic hosts, because there are no pictures, and no detailed descriptions given anywhere. All of God's angels are holy and humble, and no one can distinguish between them, but I have been able to dig deeper to bring to you what I am presenting in these pages.

DAVID'S MIGHTY MEN

To properly understand and get an idea of these angels let us take a quick look at king David's mighty men. Before there were mighty men on earth, God had created His mighty angelic beings. King David was the first king of Israel appointed by God. When he came on the scene, the JEBUSITES were a problem to Israel. He was a mighty man of war himself known for slaying thousands of people, and for slaying bears and lions with his bare hands. When he was still a fugitive from Saul he was met by thirty mighty men of the army of Israel. They declared their allegiance to him. To make a long story short, among the thirty Mighty Men were these distinguished three of them: ELEAZAR, ABISHAI, and BENAIAH. They were known for their extraordinary heights, which ranged from seven to seven and a half feet tall. They were also known for how many people and beasts they had killed. ELEAZAR was said to have killed a whole Philistine army; ABISHAI was said to have killed three hundred men. BENAIAH had killed two lion-looking heroes of Moab and a lion. These were mighty men of valor, men who did things that ordinary people could not do. You notice their power was shown in how men they killed including wild animals. These were clearly men of unmatched strength.

God created strange looking men to serve with king David. They had faces like lions, and feet like deer. They were known for their power, and for their speed in running to deliver messages. They could run hundreds of miles. They were created to root out the JEBUSITES who occupied enemy cities. King Saul did not have such people, and neither did any of the other kings in Israel's history. (1 Chronicles 25:1-12)

GOD'S MIGHTY ANGELS

When you study the Book of Revelation you get the idea that everything the apostle saw was huge, and that is exactly how things are in heaven. When God speaks it's like the heaven is going to fall off its axis. A loud trumpet sound is like ordinary speech. Things are loud, people are big, and everything is huge. He said, "then I saw another mighty angel coming down from heaven." (Revelation 10:1) It seems to me that the only word that came to the mind of the apostle when he saw this angel was the word mighty. What did he mean? The word mighty means three things: (1) a person of extraordinary height, (2) a person of great body mass, and (3) a person of supernatural strength. I want you to know that describes angelic hosts. These angels are colossal beings that defy description and they have power that is above human machines, and engines.

The bible does not list sizes and heights of these creatures, but my understanding of spirits is that they can stretch to any height and size. What the apostle was describing was a mountain of a being. I mean these are beings which can stop hurricanes and tornadoes that destroy anything in their paths. Angelic hosts have unique features which include:

a. They have voices roar like thunder;
b. They do the work of a multitudes;
c. They have appearances that cause people to tremble;
d. They can slaughter millions;
e. They have faces like the sun;
f. They have feet like pillars of fire.

ACTIVITIES OF THE HOSTS

Their power is indescribable. They are made to subdue any being in the entire universe. Scripture captures the essence of their power when it says:

> "It came to pass that night that the angel of the LORD went out and smote in the camp of the Assyrians one hundred and eighty-five thousand, and when they arose early in the morning, behold they were all dead corpses." He had only done battle for one hour. There was no telling what he would do in a whole day. Single-handedly the angel took out the whole army. (2 Kings 19:35)

While mighty men slay hundreds, mighty angels slay millions. Note that they do not get tired, and their strength is inexhaustible. *The* Lord Himself made mention of them when He was interviewed at the trial before He went to the cross by Pilate. He confirmed that His angels were fighters and created to defeat anybody and anything. In (John chapter 18:36), He stated He could request His Father to send Him twelve legions of angels. That will translate into 72,000 angels. If you multiply 72,000 by 185, 000, the minimum number that these angels would kill in a war would be over 13 billion people. That means they will wipe out the entire world and over. Note that the Lord did not come to destroy the earth. That will probably be at His Second Coming.

The information about these beings is gathered throughout the bible. You could sense that these are beings of immense sizes and power. You don't want to meet any of these anywhere.

Let us bring this even closer. About two thousand years ago Scripture says:

> "Behold, there was a great earthquake: for the angel of the Lord descended from heaven and came and **rolled back the stone** from the door and sat upon it. His countenance was like lightning and his clothes white as snow: for fear of him the keepers did tremble, and looked like dead men. And the angel answered and said unto the women, fear not ye: for I know that ye seek Jesus, Who was crucified. He is not here: for He is risen as He said. Come, and see the place where the Lord lay."
> (Matt. 28:2-6)

What do you think about this angel, and how mighty was he? The bible did not say the earthquake blew away the stone. What caused the earthquake? I don't know, but the quake was not intended to remove the stone. The angel rolled back the big boulder that would have taken a whole city to roll. The disciples' concern was this stone. Who will roll back the stone they kept asking each other? We see that this angel alone rolled back this monstrosity. That says a lot about his power.

Look at the countenance of this angel. It was like lightning and his clothes were as white as snow. He was downright scary. He was not the kind of a person you would want to meet anywhere. Scripture says the keepers trembled for fear of him. Those keepers were Roman soldiers who stood guard to make sure the Lord did not run away. How could a dead man run away?

Scripture also says there are seven mighty angels who stand at the throne of God. I believe these are all angelic hosts. Imagine how they look. As I stated above they speak with voices like thunder; they roar like lions; they do the work of a multitude; they have appearances that cause people to tremble; they slaughter hundreds of thousands, and they have tremendous power.

VIOLATORS AND ENEMIES

God's warriors do two things: (1) they fight against evil angels and Satan's followers. They also war against human violators of God's law. In both cases human beings are involved. That tells us that spiritual wars take place all the time. Most of us pray to God and God answers but getting the answers may sometimes be at a high cost battles. The forces of darkness are always there to try to impede righteous angels from carrying out God's commands. Thank God that God's angels will always be up to the task. They have done that since evil came into the universe.

We see those sometimes even in nature, such as when buildings collapse, grown-ups are killed, but a little baby is left untouched. That is the result of spiritual warfare. The devil's intention is to kill everybody, but God's angels will not allow it.

There's are cases of violent human activity. Of-course such disobedience is caused by Satan who works in the minds of people. For example, the case of king David who decided to take a census. God dispatched His angel. The angel massacred seventy thousand people. Be careful about your actions. They may just go against the LORD, and He is going to judge.

Scripture tells us of king Herod who failed to give glory to God, and we will see the persecutions of the Early Church. There are spiritual wars going on around us every day. Angelic hosts are empowered to enforce the laws of God throughout the universe. They engage violators wherever they may be. They may come to us in our dreams. That's why many people die in their sleep sometimes. Herod was being praised as a god in his party, so the angel of the LORD struck and killed him. There's a God of the universe, and you are not the one. So be careful about cases of blasphemy. His angels will hunt you down.

Summary:

As strong and powerful as angels are there are many things that link humans to angels:

> They understand that we serve the same God;
> God uses them to help us;
> We are their brethren;
> There's a celebration in heaven when a person receives Jesus Christ;
> They serve the redeemed through God;
> We have a common enemy, and that is the devil;
> Their mission and their strength is to protect he redeemed.

CHAPTER 8

God's Messengers and Servants

MESSENGER

The Psalmist said: "Bless the LORD ye Ministers of His that do His pleasure." There are two very important phrases here: "His ministers and do His pleasure." (Psalm 103:21) We are going to use this verse with everything we discuss in this chapter. In the first place this is what angels do: They are committed to serve God with everything they have.

The verse of Scripture listed above says angels are God's messengers or ministers. A minister is defined as a servant, a voluntary attendant, and one who performs the services of God. We may call them some other things, but the most important duty of an angel is a **messenger**. It seems to me that there are only two types of jobs in heaven: God's position, and the servant position. That makes the job of an angel very important.

Angels take their job very seriously for the following reasons: (1) they get to be in the presence of God all the time, (2) they have an opportunity to see His face all the time, and (3) they get to learn of His ways. That means everything.

What I just said there can be compared to the time when the Lord Jesus went to Mary and Martha's house. Mary could not leave the sight of the Lord. He was her choice; but Martha, her sister, was busy with other things. Then she turned around and blamed her sister for sitting around with the Lord and doing nothing. "Only one thing really matters, and that is Mary has chosen the right thing." the Lord told Martha. There are any number of things that angels could choose, but they have chosen to serve the LORD with everything they have, and there's absolutely nothing greater than that.

With humans a messenger is often the least of the jobs, and no one wants to be associated with such a job. Heaven is a very different place. Maybe there are other jobs there, and maybe not, but angels have chosen the right one as mentioned above. I think that is very important, because they get to see the Lord, they get to be in His presence, and they get to learn of His ways, they get to learn of His will, and they get to be sent to perform duties for the Most- High God. That's awesome.

An angels is a trusted servant of God. That makes all the difference. As a servant he is counted upon to carry the Almighty's messages, see His secrets, and to know His business. That is a very important responsibility. Not everyone can do this job. As we know some angels had left their first estate and were cast out of heaven forever. That was because the LORD could not trust them. Some of them are now in the abyss. They are now lower than humans. For one thing they can never come before the LORD ever again. That is their worst loss ever.

It means the world to be trusted by God. Angels are like the link between heaven and humans. For example, they were the first to bring word concerning the Incarnation of our Lord Jesus Christ, and about His birth. They were the first at His Resurrection. They have the reputation that the LORD trusts them completely. Can you imagine that if the president of the USA wants to send anybody somewhere he says, get me Ralph or John? It is personal, because if the Most -High wants to send anybody, He calls those He trusts, and that is His angel.

Scripture says messengers are created to serve God willingly, attending to whatever pleases Him. No one could have put it more succinctly than the great king David when he said: "Bless the LORD ye Ministers of His that do His pleasure." (Psalm 103:21) The last part of that statement is equally as important, because doing His pleasure is what describes the job of a messenger. That means they give themselves to the job. When you consider the fact that they are working for their maker it makes much more sense. If your Master is not pleased with your work you may not have a job very long, but the Almighty loves the work of His angels.

In the broader context of our definition a messenger is one who is **sent**. That also means one who obeys to do whatever he is sent to do. In other words, the primary meaning of a messenger is to obey God unquestionably. They are sent to serve lowly mankind, sometimes babies trapped in accidents, etc., no matter where they are sent their answer has always been the same: "Lord send me." I find that very humbling, and that's why I am writing about angels. In doing their job they get to know the business of the Almighty.

LORD SEND ME

This answer has been given before by the prophet Isaiah, when the LORD asked, "whom shall I send, and who will go for us." He said, "Lord, send me." (Isaiah 6:8) This is perhaps the greatest answer that anyone should have when it comes to the call of God. I believe this should be our prayer. I have heard many preachers tell their congregation members to dream big. That is completely missing the point. You and I have no ability to dream. I know that because I am a dreamer, and only God can give us dreams. God can cause us to dream, because He knows the places where He wants to take us. Secondly, you can't ask God to give you dreams, because God's dreams span through thousands of years, so you might not live to see what you ask for. Joseph was a dreamer and he died in Egypt, and at that time his dreams had just started. God can dream big, because He lives forever.

Again, our greatest prayer should be Lord send me to wherever You want me to go. He might send you wherever He wants you to go which is usually the destination of your calling. If you do a good job, then you become someone He can trust. The Lord Himself said, "you are My friends if you do what I have commanded you to do." (John 15:14) Remember there's a condition there. The condition is "if you do what I have commanded you." Abraham became God's friend, not because he was equal with God, but because he served God humbly. When the LORD called him He replied kneeling down, "Your servant is listening!" You remember when the LORD came to his door, he bowed down before Him, and begged the LORD to eat at his tent before leaving. And He fetched water to wash Their Feet before leaving. If you want God to use you, offer yourself humbly to Him and say, "LORD send me." Let me give you a secret: when you are like Abram you go from slave to a friend of God. What a man! God treats His angels as if they were His friends because they serve so well.

SERVICE IS THEIR REWARD

The service of angels is their reward. No matter where they are, angels always serve with grace. When they come to us, and as glorious as they may be, they always say: "I am sent." I find that absolutely humbling. No wonder the Lord said unless you become children you cannot be my disciple. An angel is like that good child who, forever never grows up, or mature into a grown man, because of his humility. That is my view. They forever voluntarily and intentionally give of themselves to obeying and carrying out instructions and commands of their Master. I love it, and that's also why I am writing this book.

They take no glory for what they do. They are like their Master, the Lord Jesus, who made Himself of no reputation, and they do not hesitate to give glory to God, the One who deserves all the honor and glory for anything they do. They understand the gap between them and their Master, and they serve Him with everything they have. *I don't think we understand that difference today.* They realize that the Almighty deserves all their services. The earlier we understand that the better we become better servants like the holy angels of God.

HUMBLE SERVANT

The greatest virtue of an angel, in my view, is humility. This was exemplified by our Lord Jesus Christ Himself when He walked the earth and died on the cross for us. His angels follow His example. They are as selfless as their Master. It seems as if humility is written in their training manual, so to speak. Sometimes I wonder why God even bothers with us. I think He sees something in us that I can never see. We do not really qualify for His great ministry. The first couple failed Him miserably. Of course, it is not a matter of qualifications, it is a matter of His great love for us. He gives us chances, because, "it is not in His will that any should perish." As soon as we demonstrate humility the good Lord can use us. To understand humility, let us look at our Lord's life as spelt out in scripture:

> **"Let this mind be in you which was also in Christ Jesus: who, being in the very nature of God, but he did not con- sider equality with God, but made Himself of no reputation, and took upon Himself the form of a a servant, and was made in the likeness of men: as a man He humbled Himself and became obedient unto death, even the death of a cross."** (Philippians 2:5-8)

Each time I read this passage I just weep. Considering Who He is, and what He did for us was just exemplary. No human could do that. In summary, He is God, but did not consider Himself equal with God. He humbled Himself and took human nature (a slave). As a man He obeyed His Father and became a servant, and as a Servant He was obedient to death, and death on a cross, meant for thieves and bad people. He went down five levels of humility. That was Incredible! We could never thank Him enough. Having read what our Lord went through I can summarize it into the following statement:

Humility requires that we become obedient to another person, a superior, or inferior person to us. Our Lord had to obey His Father's commands to come to earth. He took human form, and He died. He could have not accomplished this goal, if He insisted on being a Divine Figure, or if He exercised His rights as God. In obeying he lay down His life for us. What a Savior!

Self-sacrifice is one of those things that you must do to become a humble servant. We have seen that He sacrificed His divine nature and became a man. Being a man has its own challenges. The Lord had to undergo those challenges. By His very nature He was imperishable, but he sacrificed that too. Basically, He became a created being. Being God was a luxury He should not have given up, but He loved us too much. To be humble you consider the interests of others before yours. We were on His mind as He went to that cross. He knew that if He did not do it we could not do it ourselves. So, He went to the cross knowing fully well what He was doing, but He did it anyway. He understood the disgrace, the humiliation, the torment, the insults, the taunts by those who taunted Him. In doing so He put our interests above His.

Becoming humble He accepted what I call the door-mat-syndrome. The door-mat syndrome means giving yourself to be used as a doormat for the good of others. In other words, He accepted the lowest possible outcome which is, He could become the lowest of the lowest to make others better. Considering where He came from most of us in America would say, "I have my pride." That was the last thing on His mind. In fact, He had no pride. This is the whole idea: humility is the complete erosion of pride. Our Lord was the humblest servant of all.

SERVANTHOOD

Servant-hood can sometimes be construed as slavery here on earth and it was recognized in Jewish society under three circumstances: (1) poverty: when a man becomes unable to support his family; (2) commission of theft; and (3) the exercise of paternal authority where the person offers his daughter for sale.

Termination of slavery for those involved according to the law:

1. ended after six years;
2. termination also ended with the death of the slave master;
3. in the years of the Jubilee.

With that in mind the service of angels cannot be construed as any kind of slavery, because they are God's servants and life on earth is not like life in heaven. In fact, the service of angels is a noble service, because they are already in the service of the Almighty God.

SERVING WITH INTENTIONALITY

The angel's action in knocking out king Herod was intentional or with purpose. He saw the opportunity in a man who regarded himself as god and he took it. (Acts 12:23) That is the same thing they do in their work, they are very intentional. They enforce God's law as soon as they see an opportunity. To be intentional also means to be aggressive. The call of God is urgent, because time is not waiting for any of us. We must decide quickly. The devil is not waiting for us either, he can throw many ideas at us to make us change our mind. A friend came to me one day and said, "do you know what, I have been called to serve the Lord too." I responded, "oh yea, where are you serving." He said, "I want to go to school first." That's not where the Lord sent him. To serve God must be intentional, or aggressive, if you will. If He calls, we must leave now. In other words, we must be sold out by God. I like what the prophet Elisha did when God called him. He went and sold his farm, and the cattle, and cooked some of the cattle, and invited his friends and they ate, and he left. Angels are made to serve at a moment's notice. You can't let the enemy bring in different ideas. Act right away.

Serving with intentionality also means taking deliberate action in serving God. Angels are deliberate in their work. We can't let adverse conditions and other things stop us. We must move on with what God has called us unless He says otherwise. Angels serve with determination and dedication.

SERVING WITH EXHILARATION

The word exhilaration means expressing liveliness or excitement in performing a task. Angels are excited in their work. When Gabriel came to Mary he was lively and excited in the delivery of the divine message. Angels love their work, and they do it with excitement, because it is an opportunity. There are trillions of angels in heaven eager to serve. Gabriel delivered the message of the advent of Christ with exhilaration. It seemed as if he was watching the baby Jesus from heaven while he spoke to Mary saying: "Behold you shall conceive in your womb and shall bring forth a son." What woman would not like to hear that kind of news, especially to bear the Son of God?

Gabriel's work paid off. See how Mary reacted after Gabriel finished:

"Be it unto me according to thy word, or I accept it."
(Luke 1:38)

The Gospel is good news, the best news ever known, but we are so caught up with our earthly problems that sometimes we forget to enjoy what the Word of God says, or what He is trying to tell us on any given day. In those days it was the only Word of the Day. When the man of God Moses spoke, people stood at the door of their tents. They dropped whatever they were doing and listened.

This book is all about bringing out the excitement of what the LORD has given us to do. Every preacher out there should preach the word of God's excitement. There's no other way out, because whatever God says is going to happen, as it did after Gabriel spoke to Mary. The Lord was born, and He changed the world for every human forever.

Bringing the message with life makes all the difference. That way the listener sees it as if it is happening right now. Gabriel said, "behold" which means look, as if the event was within his view. This transports the listener by faith to what the deliverer is talking about. In fact, it turns the message into reality. Now the listener is no longer just listening to a story, but he or she is transported mentally to where the event is occurring. That is serving with exhilaration.

SERVING WITH DILIGENCE

Angels serve with diligence which is carefully weighing their choices and options. God expects us to exercise diligence in the things we do. His angels do His work with careful attention to details, and with excellence. Scripture exhorts us all to be diligent in anything we do. There are many choices in life, too many roads to travel, and too many things to choose from. We have an enemy who is presenting us with wrong choices to trip us up. We must be diligent in making those choices.

Angels do their work diligently. They listen to the tone of the Lord's voice to make sure they understand what the Lord is saying. That's just like the servants of the Lord. There's no room for mistakes. They are careful and methodical in assessing the task that the LORD has given.

Scripture also speaks of the word command. First a command is an imperative statement. It is not asking for your opinion. It is demanding that you do what is being commanded. A command is usually given by a king. When the king gives his command, he expects his subjects to obey it and carry it out thoroughly. In most cases commandments are laws. That's what they stand for biblically speaking.

God is our King of the universe. From what we know about Him He knows everything, He has all power, He is Mightier than we could ever imagine. I mean there's no word to properly describe who God is. Having said that, we should understand what His commands mean, and act with diligence.

FERVENT WORSHIPPERS

Angels worship with fervency. That means worshiping with passion, and intensity. Scripture says angels worship God day and night, seven days a week, four weeks per month, twelve months per year, and forever and forever. In doing so, they give of themselves to it. Think about it! I know that it is impossible for us humans to have the power and energy to worship as long as angels do. That's why they are supernatural beings. The Isaiah version says: "One cried to another and said, Holy, Holy." That is a duet.

The Revelation of worship says:

> **"holy, holy, holy;**
> **is the LORD God Almighty;**
> **who was, and is, and is to come."** (Revelation 4:8;
> Isaiah 6:3)

It shows the intensity of it. No human being can worship like the angels of God. Scripture says "day, and night, and forever and ever they do not stop worshiping. That's fervency.

DOING HIS PLEASURE

In conclusion angels do whatever pleases God. The question becomes: what pleases the Almighty? Basically, it is what we have been discussing in this chapter. The Almighty is pleased by the following:

A. Those who serve Him humbly;
B. Those who serve with excitement;
C. Those who give themselves to serve Him;
D. Those who serve with diligence;
E. Fervent worshippers.

As we said above angels are the humblest worshippers. Glorious as they are, they will give anything to be humble to their Master. As I mentioned earlier, God does not need us. He has the best service anywhere in His angelic servants. They serve Him with joy and excitement. They are not forced to do it, but they give of themselves willingly. It is not like let us do it for the job, but they are happy doing it. They live to serve their Master, because they are nothing without their duty to Him.

They give of themselves to serve. It seems to me that every angel knows that the others are dying to serve. So, it is a chance, and an opportunity of a lifetime to serve the Most- High. No one wants to miss that golden chance. When you understand who the Most- High is, you die serving.

They serve with diligence. On their list of things to do on a given day, serving the Most high remains the highest and everyone is dying to do that. Finally, they serve with fervency. They do it round the clock, and forever and ever. They never get tired, and hunger and thirst are not their problem. Our machines may break down, but the angelic system of service lasts forever.

CHAPTER 9

The Resurrection

RAISING LAZARUS

S hortly before His death the Lord raised a man from the dead by the name of Lazarus. The man and his sisters were the Lord's friends from the town of Bethany in Judea. Addressing a watching crowd when asked by the dead man's family who apparently knew that the resurrection will happen at the Last Day, the Lord stepped forward and shouted:

> "I AM THE RESURRECTION, AND THE LIFE.
> HE WHO BELIEVES IN ME EVEN IF HE
> WERE dead yet SHALL HE LIVE." (John 11:25)

That was a bold claim. The fact is He was going to make it come true. You see He was told about the man's sickness, but He waited until the man died, and was buried. In, fact scripture tells us that the man was buried four days before the Lord showed up. When you are God **all things** work according to your will. He can come in whenever He wants. He has all power and all things obey Him. Consequently, any time He comes is always the right time. Though Mary and her sister Marta worried, they could not change anything. The Lord's time is always the right time. Then the Lord stepped into the place where the dead man lay, and called him out with a shout:

"LAZARUS COME FORTH." (John 11:25)

His voice penetrated the depths of the earth and raised the dead and rotting man back to life. A voice that would have raised millions, this was no ordinary voice, it was the voice of **Power, and might, the voice of God.** That was the voice of the Almighty God, the Giver of life. When Lazarus heard he received life and strength and knew that it was the voice of his Master. He recognized that **unique** voice and call from deep yonder, the unsearchable reaches of the dead. It penetrated the earth to break the power of death.

The frightened and cheering crowd, not sure of what to make of this, shouted with their hands in their mouths: **What kind of man is this** they asked, in disbelief? No one had ever done this sort of thing since the dawn of human history. Some cried out, and many were leaping for joy at what was taking place.

The confused crowd was filled with all kinds of emotions as the Son of the Highest went to work. The incident stuck in the minds of those who watched, not able to decide whether they were watching a movie or an actual event. Raising Lazarus would have left no doubt in the minds of onlookers that He Himself would rise again, but it didn't.

RESURRECTION FORETOLD

Before His arrest the Lord had told His disciples at least two times these words:

> "I must go to Jerusalem, and suffer many things
> At the hands of the elders and chief priests and
> Scribes and be killed and rise again on the third day."
> (Matthew 16:21).

Again, He said:

> We are going up to Jerusalem, and the Son
> of Man will be betrayed to the chief priests
> and the teachers of the law. They will condemn

Him to death and they will turn Him over to the
Gentiles to be mocked, flogged and He will be crucified.
On the third day He will be raised to life."
(Matthew 20:17-19)

As He spoke the words entered one ear and came out of the other of
the disciples. Why? I believe for the following reasons:

No one has ever risen from the dead, so this could not happen;
They forgot all His other miracles that He had done;
They forgot that He recently raised Lazarus from the
dead;
They forgot that He was The Son of the Living God as
Peter declared;
They chose to follow what everybody was saying;
They forgot that nothing is too hard for God, including
the Son of God.

The disciples joined the list of doubters: the chief priests, the teachers
of the law, fulfilling scripture which said:

He was despised and rejected of men;
a man of sorrows, and acquainted with grief:
and we hid as it were our faces from Him;
He was despised, and we esteemed Him not.
(Isaiah 53:3)

He was rejected by those He came to save, including even the most
devout of them - Mary Magdalene. The disciples may have forgotten, or
did not believe, but there was another group of His own servants who
heard the same message, and they knew that the grave could not hold
Him. These were His angels.

DEATH AND BURIAL

The Resurrections is the process by which someone who is dead and buried comes back from the dead. In this case the **someone was none other than our Mighty Lord Jesus Christ**. He was Tortured, beaten beyond recognition, crucified, died, and was buried, and on the third day He rose from the dead. This event is one of the most contested and most important events of our faith, but what most people forget is that this was not an event that was left to man. Heaven was the first presence of the Incarnation.

The Lord died a very cruel death. He was bruised, meaning He was beaten beyond recognition and thousands saw Him die. Roman soldiers made sure this One who claimed to be God received the maximum punishment. I mean the devil did a job in terms of physical beating. A crown of thorns was placed on His head. Those thorns caused Him to bleed all the way to the cross. Add the soldiers who whipped on both sides, don't forget the mockers, and those who spat on Him from all sides. By the time He was handed to the last batch of tormentors He looked like a Person upon whom a truck had run over. The last golden words He uttered were, **"it is finished." (John 19:30).** With those words He bowed His head and breathed His last.

These were not empty words. Those words meant that He had finished the **requirements for sin** for human redemption forever. They signified the reason why He came. That's why He took human form, that's why He suffered. The price for our sin was so great, and for some of us we will praise him forever and ever. His name shall be on our lips and on our hearts as the greatest Name ever known.

What does it mean to die? Most people have different thoughts about death. I am not a doctor, and I have not been dead yet, but I know a few things about death. To die means permanent loss of memory, brain function, and all body parts cease to function. Everything that keeps a person alive comes to a total halt. You don't recognize children, relatives, etc., even if they are standing in front of you. Death is the complete cessation of life. Those who say their loved ones are watching over them after they pass on do not understand death. If you could not function, you surely are not going to watch others after you buried.

The Lord had completed the death process. All the parts of His body were dead, and when He breathed His last he was dead. A tomb was prepared, and a boulder that was placed on the door of the tomb. As if this was not enough, a band of Roman soldiers was selected to watch over the tomb. The soldiers took turns watching the tomb. The idea was to make sure that no power on earth would move the stone.

This boulder was the thing that was on the apostles' minds: "who will remove the stone?" Thousands watched the Lord's body taken from the cruel cross, and placed in the tomb, as He pronounced those words: "it is finished." Others watched as the women struggled day by day to apply burial oils on the body of the Holy One.

It was settled in the mind of the devil that the Lord had gone the way of other men since the beginning of man's curse of death. He was satisfied with having avenged his self-proclaimed enemy by doing away with the Son of God whom he knew very well.

For all people, death leaves *a gaping hole in the hearts those who have lost a loved one.* For some of us it feels like the sting never goes away and nothing in the world could fill that hole. The disciples were crushed by the death of their Beloved Master. As for Mary Magdalene she never stopped weeping, and she wept her way right to the day of the Resurrection with the Lord standing right beside her. Those tears however, were tears of unbelief. The rest of them were very confused wondering about what would become of their own lives from then on? They had come to believe that nothing like this would happen to their beloved Master. Until then many had refused to believe the words of the Master that **He would rise again time and time again.** The Devil on his part had no clue about the Resurrection. Those who say Satan is the wisest angel, how could he not know that he was fulfilling the will of God by putting Christ to death?

ANGELS WITNESS THE RESURRECTION

Nobody knows exactly when the angels got there, but biblical accounts of the Resurrection reveal they were the first on the scene of this momentous event. They heard the Lord's speech when He mentioned that He will die and be buried, and on the third day rise again. They took it to heart, and they knew that the grave could not hold Him, so they acted on it.

MATTHEW'S GOSPEL

"The angel of the Lord came down from heaven, rolled back the stone and sat on it. This angel was clearly an angelic host. He was very powerful. He rolled back the stone alone. The stone was so large that all the disciples feared they could not roll it. His appearance was like lightning and his clothes as white as snow. This is one of those angels who could do the work of thousands. The guards were so afraid of him that they trembled at his sight of him. They fell down and became like dead men." The angel said to the women, "don't be afraid, for I know that you are looking for Jesus who was crucified. He is not here. He has risen as He said. (Matthew. 28:2-6)

MARK'S GOSPEL

"As the disciples entered the tomb they saw that the tomb had been rolled, but they saw a young man in white clothing, (an angel) sitting on the right side, and they were alarmed." "Don't be alarmed," he said, "you are looking for Jesus, the Nazarene who was crucified. He is not here. He is risen." (Mark 16:6)

LUKE'S GOSPEL

"While the disciples were wondering where the body of the Lord was there stood beside them two men (angels) in clothes that **shone like**

lightning (angelic host), and they said: "Why do you look for the living among the dead?" He is not here; He is risen." Luke 24:4 Remember how He told you while He was still with you in Galilee: "the Son of Man must be delivered into the hands of sinful men, be crucified and on the third day be raised again." (Luke 18:32-33)

JOHN'S GOSPEL

Mary Magdalene came weeping for the body of her Master even though the Lord was standing right there asking: "woman, why are you weeping?" This is a form of hypocrisy. Those were tears of unbelief, because Mary must have heard the speech that the Lord gave stating that He would rise again. The Lord's question implied: "Why are you weeing? That was to say, this is not the time to weep. This is the time to rejoice. I told you guys I will rise again, and here I am." He asked, "Whom seek ye?" Again, He meant, "this is not the time to bring embalming fluids, I am not dead I am alive." (John 20:15) She thought the Lord was one of the farmers until He called her name, "Mary." Then she recognized the voice of the Master and she cried out in Aramaic: "RABBONI." (John 20:16)

Mary's response is so important, because it shuts up the naysayers of the Resurrection. Even rising from the dead after three days, His voice remained the same. As I said in my first book, a person can recognize the voice of another person even if all other parts of the body are destroyed. Mary's answer was one of the greatest proofs of the Resurrection of our Lord. To recognize the Lord's voice after He rose from the dead is nothing short of a miracle.

These statements and questions caught the disciples by surprise, turning the occasion which was supposed to be a joyous one, into one of disbelief, and shock. No one was seen jumping around because of what had happened. I think it was strange to them, because they had never seen anything like this, even though He had told them He would rise again many times. I believe the disciples needed time to process this idea of Him coming back, even though they had wept, and regretted His death.

The angels never forgot what He had told them concerning His rising again, and when time came they were there. God had His witness in His angels to this very important event. You have heard that more than five hundred people saw Him when He rose, but the most important truth is that His angels were the first witnesses of the Resurrection. No matter how much disbelief there might have been concerning the event the most important thing was that it was witness and recorded in heaven. This is the difference between angels and us humans. They live for their Lord. His words are their life. They heard and remembered what He said, and it stuck with them. When the time came they were there to see Him rise.

The angel rolled back the stone from the tomb where the Lord was buried. This angel was mighty and powerful to be able to move that massive stone. The earthquake did not roll the stone, the angel did it alone. The noise made by the stone as it was tossed away sounded like a quake. The concern of the disciples was about this massive stone at the entrance of the tomb. It made it difficult for them to get to the tomb. That was because they forgot that their Master was going to rise again. The important point was that an actual burial of the Lord took place. He went down on a Friday afternoon, and rose early in the morning on Sunday. He was in the bowels of the earth for three days as He said.

REMOVING THE STING OF DEATH

As you can see all of us who have received the Savior are still dying: meaning we are still suffering from the first level of the sting of death. That is alright, because Christ has guaranteed that you and I will not see that second death. That's where it really counts. Removing the sting of death does two things for us:

1. Man will never die again;
2. Our names are written in Lamb's Book Life.

MAN WILL NEVER DIE AGAIN

In the west and other parts of the people still believe that after people die they go to some type of heaven. They conjured up ideas that their loved ones are still in their graves or are somewhere watching the living. The bible does not teach that. Those are tricks of the devil to prevent people from receiving the Lord Jesus. The Resurrection assures that that we will never die again.

The truth is once you die you die, and there's no power that can bring you back. Christ is the only One who can do that. He is our only answer. Invite the Lord into your heart so your name can be written in what we call the Lamb's Book of Life, and you will have everlasting life. Your name will be written there so you can be found by your loved ones. If the name is not written there then you are lost forever. As you and I mourn for our people the devil is having a party, but if their names are not written in the Book of Life his party will be over.

LAMB'S BOOK OF LIFE

So, believe on the Lord Jesus Christ, and you and your loved ones will be saved and will spend eternity with Christ. When that happens, your names are written in the Lamb's Book of Life. (Revelation 20:12) That is the importance of the Resurrection of Christ. You can see that all of us who have received the Savior are still dying. That means we are still suffering from the first level of death. We can deal with that, because flesh and blood cannot enter the kingdom of heaven anyway. For us Christ has guaranteed we won't see that second death. That's where it counts.

The Resurrection was the ultimate test for our Lord. No one knew that a man could ever conquer death, but Christ did it. The devil threw all his energy in nailing Jesus to that cross, but he forgot that Christ was the Creator of life. When time came Jesus proved to the devil and to the world that He was Who He said He was. That tells me that the devil is not as smart as he thinks he is. The word of God puts it this way:

"Howbeit we speak wisdom among them that
Are perfect: yet not the wisdom of this world,
Nor of the princes of this world, that come to
Nothing: but we speak the wisdom of God
In a mystery, that is the hidden wisdom
Which God ordained before the world unto
Our glory: which none of the princes of this
World knew, for had they known they would
Not have crucified the Lord of glory." (I Corinthians.
2:6-8)

That wisdom is the word of God. It seems to me that God spoke in tongues, so that the devil would not understand. Even if he heard it he did not know how God would become a man to die and rise from the dead in order to save mankind. When the Lord rose from the dead, the devil was lost, and confused. That is the difference between the devil and the Creator of all things. Alleluia to the Lord of glory. As He saved us our names are written in the Lamb's Book of Life which is a Register for the living.

CHRIST THE LORD

The goal of this book is to confirm that Jesus Christ is the same God of the universe of yesteryears whom the angels called Christ the LORD. The Resurrections confirms that. Christians all over the globe recognize the resurrection of Christ as concrete proof of His Divinity. It proves that He has power over death because only God has power over death. Anybody who has defeated death cannot die and therefore He lives forever. Jesus Christ has done that, and He is the Lord and God of the universe.

THE POWER OF THE GOSPEL

The message of the Cross and Resurrection is very clear: Jesus Christ returned to life from the dead they say. These events are the Most important events in Christianity. Since man sinned and sin entered the world men have been dying as God said: "the soul that sins shall die." No one has ever died and returned. And for centuries generations of the sons of men have suffered from the sting of death.

It seems as if the Father spoke to the Son about the Resurrection and it was carried out. That way the devil was lost. He did not understand that there was a resurrection. You see when Satan saw the Lord Jesus on earth he thought the Lord came to shorten his time or he simply did not know what to think. You see he fought hard to crucify the Lord Jesus thinking the Lord was just another man who will go the way of other men. So, after the resurrection happened, the devil was dumbfounded. He learned like everyone else about it but then it was too late. He screamed in ignorance. He did not understand the manifold wisdom of God. When the Lord is about to begin serious matters, it seems the devil is always left out of the loop. This the one they say he is so wise. I don't think. Sin does that you.

He promised His followers: disciples, and angels that no one could stop Him. That's the same thing that happened when the LORD sent plagues to Egypt. At first the plagues were simple things that Satan could duplicate, but the LORD was just beginning. When things got heated up the devil was lost. Folks the devil is the one who has fallen not us.

In summary, when the enemy put the Lord on the Cross he thought he got Him on the ropes. It turned out to be a very big mistake, for the devil had no clue of the Resurrection. Satan thought he had dealt the final blow on Christ as He did to the sons of men. This time he did it to One far superior to himself. Therefore, Christ is Lord, and God of the Universe. He is invincible, and He is above death. He defeated the power of sin and death. Those who have sinned and come to Him in repentance can be forgiven. This victory has been extended to the believers of Christ all over the world.

The power and wisdom of God made the Resurrection so easy. The Lord was under the Earth three days. It was as if He went to sleep one day and got up the next day. He was fine by all scientific measures, but it was something no human being can even attempt to accomplish. That's why no one has ever come back the way the Lord did. Death leaves you dead, that means all the body dies. What the Lord did is simply the greatest miracle. Only God can defeat death, therefore the resurrection confirms that Jesus Christ is God.

We know all too well of people who have suffered from traumatic situations: fatal accidents, plane crashes, fatal gunshots, etc. They usually remain brain-dead or stay in a comma for the rest of their lives. At times after survival from death they remain at a vegetative state, and they may not survive. Let us examine how our Lord did after rising from the dead.

EVIDENCE OF THE RESURRECTION

I am not a medical doctor and I know nothing about human anatomy and physiology. Evidence is a personal assessment of the performance of the Lord right after rising from the dead. This evidence is gathered from the pages of the holy word of God. It is impossible for anyone to come back from the dead. That's why we have lost billions of people since Adam fell. It is only in the Bible that we see people who have never died at all, and it is from there that we see people raised from the dead. It is from the Bible that the Lord discussed His resurrection, and it happened exactly as He said.

After He rose from the dead He had a dual personality, in what we call a glorified body, able to appear, and disappear. He did other miraculous things so, evidence discusses His supernatural abilities to function in ways that totally defy comprehension.

PHYSICAL APPEARANCE

In John's Gospel we see the Lord standing among His angels. He looked like one of the farmers. He was standing with them. Looking at Him interact with them we know that He maintained His normal physical form with no lacerations, death marks, etc. The resurrection is a mystery of unparalleled proportions. We know that people who come from a near-death experience remain in a vegetative state the rest of their lives, not being to speak, let alone resume their normal form. Only God would do the things our Lord did. NORMAL COMMUNICATION

When the Lord rose, scriptures says He was communicating normally with His disciples. He asked Mary Magdalene: "why are you weeping." By this He meant, should you not be rejoicing now? I am the One talking to you. People heard Him and when they talked, He understood responded perfectly. There was nothing questionable about His ability to understand. I tell you people who come back from the dead generally lose communicable and other abilities, but that was not the case with our Lord. Usually those who have a near-death are trained and retrained to talk, and their speech remains altered the rest of their life. Most of them remain partially brain-dead. They go through extensive speech therapies, but to no avail. ever did that. The Lord's case was exceptional. He resumed communication right away. He was perfect. Nobody has ever done this.

HE KNEW THEIR NAMES

Concerning communication, He was perfect. He called Mary by name: "**Mary.**" At the mention of her name, Mary recognized the voice and responded with, "RABBONI, meaning Master. Normal people who have suffered from traumas will not even speak, let alone know peoples' names.

Sometimes, they would just stare at the person or into space. After years of therapy then they perhaps start learning how to pronounce names. Most people get taught to pronounce words or speak like little children. They may go through speech therapy and other therapies, in order recover in brain function which the never do.

Some never do recover from the experience. The Lord had no problem speaking and pronouncing words. His ability to speak was completely phenomenal.

BRAIN FUNCTION

His brain function was astronomical. For someone who just rose from the dead He was unbelievable. It was like He just got up from sleep. He knew where He was, and who He was with. He resumed with supernormal brain function. Being able to communicate with people and knowing His disciples' names gave is the understanding that He was more human. Normal people would be brain dead or at a vegetative brain level. His responses and communication were supernatural.

HE GAVE THEM THE HOLY SPIRIT

After the Lord rose He made two appearances to His disciples. The first time Thomas was not with them. He seemed to be operating in the spirit and in human form. When He appeared to them the doors were closed, but He just appeared between them, without breaking doors or tearing down the roofs. He breathed on His them saying:

"Receive ye the Holy spirit. Whosoever sins you remit they are remitted unto them, and whosoever sins you retain they are retained." With that the disciples became Christians at once.

HE HAD BREAKFAST

The next thing that the Lord did was asking His disciples: "Children, have ye any meat? Their answer was obviously, no food. They were out fishing. There were obvious things with Him that showed that He was now Man and Spirit. (1) He could appear and disappear. (2) He could appear at any place they were without coming through the doors or even knocking. This time He wanted food. The question was, "how does a man who has risen from the dead eat right away?" He was Man and Spirit, how does such He eat? Where does He put the food?

We know that He was fully human. We see Him as a Person. We see His face and Thomas put his hands through His side, before believing. As a Person He could eat so, He ate breakfast with His disciples.

HE RESUMED MINISTRY

The disciples had gone fishing, but they returned without making any catch so, the Lord went right to work saying:

"Cast the net on the right side of the ship and ye shall find." (John 21:6)

When they did they had an unbelievable catch, and once again they were unable to pull their nets into the boat. They had to invite other boats to help them with the catch. That brought memories of the first catch where they were called to follow Him. He had resumed ministry work as He continued with miracles.

RESTORING PETER

As the disciples got convinced that it was their Lord Jesus He called Peter to the side, and pronounced the famous:

Peter do you love me more than these, feed my lambs;
Peter do you love me more these, feet my sheep;
Peter do you love me more than these, feed my sheep.

Why He would ask these questions, no one really knew, but Peter knew that he had failed the Lord as a leader when he denied Him. Even Thomas told him that. There was no reason to believe he (Peter) would do any better. But God is powerful, and He knows the end of all us. He has so much power that He toys with us, and if we fool around He can give us the ropes to hang ourselves. The Lord who is omniscient went on to restore Peter as the leader of the church. Some disciples were not too happy about that, but the Lord made His decision and He never made mistakes.

Peter has been one who shoots his mouth all the time. If you read the bible you'd see that he was not as excited as his brother Andrew when he was called, yet the Lord made him the leader saying: "I will make you fisher of men," in that miraculous catch of fish. He was the same one who said that even if everyone denied the Lord he would not do so. He is the same one who cut off the ear of one of the soldiers when the Lord was arrested. It was the same Peter who continued with his bigotry until the Lord dropped a plate of food from heaven telling him:

> "Arise, Peter, slay and eat." And Peter said:
> "Not so Lord: for nothing common or unclean had at any time entered into my mouth." The voice answered again from heaven, "What God had cleansed, that call not unclean." That was done three times. Immediately three gentiles were sent by the Spirit and Peter was to go with them without doubting." He continued in his racism which almost destroyed the church. It seems to me that his mistakes almost caused him to lose his position in the church as Paul was given the New Covenant instead. (Acts 11:7-12)

Having said that, Peter was like all of us, because we all make mistakes and the Lord knew that. That's the neat thing about our Lord. No matter what we do, if we confess He will always forgive us. That is the heart of God. When the Lord died, Peter did not throw in the towel. He knew that he had blundered in his role as leader, but he stuck around, because he also knew that his Lord would forgive him. Thanks be to the LORD for the great love with which He has loved us. Amen.

CLOSING REMARKS

Scripture tells us that God raised His Son from the dead. So, the Credit of all this goes to God, who made sure He kept His promise in doing this. He had to, there was too much at stake. Right after Adam failed God made this plan: to let Christ die, and to raise Him from the dead. Of course, our lives depend on it. A great part of the credit also goes to His angels who knew that death could not hold Him down. We might argue all we want here on earth, but the Incarnation is stored up in God's archives in heaven for ever.

CHAPTER 10

Angels and The Church

THE NEW CHURCH

The church is not a human institution. It is not a place for any kind of gatherings. It belongs to Jesus Christ. Before Christ there was no Church, and the word did not exist at all. The church is the product of the Cross, because the Lord shed His blood on it and the church came forth. Many keep arguing who the head of the church is. The answer is simple, and that is the One who died on that Cross. The Lord had to die to atone for our sins, and after death He rose from the dead then the church came forth. You don't have a church unless a person died, and rose from the dead, and there is only one person who did that and His name is the Lord Jesus Christ.

There were, other religious institution before Christ, but the Mission of the Lord on earth was not to establish another religion, but to bring forth what He called the church. When He started His Ministry, He began to teach His disciples and to send them out to preach saying: "repent for the kingdom of God has come upon you. (Matthew. 4:17) They did not quite understand what He was teaching.

After the disciples returned from a preaching trip one day He called them together and asked them these two questions: "Who do men say that I the Son of Man, AM?" (Matthew 16:14) Some off-the-wall answers went up. Secondly, He asked them again, "But who do you say that I

AM?" (Matthew 16:15) A deep silence swept the room. Then Simon jumped up and said, "You are the Christ, the Son of the Living God." There was another silence. Then the Master Himself said:

> "Flesh and blood have not revealed this to
> You but by My Father who is in heaven.
> Peter, upon this rock I will build MY Church, and the
> Gates of hades shall not prevail against it. (Matthew16:18)
> I will give unto you the keys of the kingdom of
> Heaven; whatever you bind on earth will
> Be bound in heaven, and whatever you lose on
> Earth will be loosed in heaven." **(Matthew16:17-19)**

Peter was a calling name that the Lord Himself gave Simon, and the meaning of that name is a rock. So, the Lord was speaking to the name, the rock upon which He would build His church. Simon did not understand what the Lord was talking about. It was a word of revelation from God the Father that just popped out of Simon's head. I am not sure that even he knew what he was saying.

That was the first time anyone heard of the word Church. So, the church is a word that came straight from the mouth of the Lord Jesus Christ. Nobody understood what it meant. To make a long story short, the Church is founded upon the Revealed Word of God through Simon. He had absolutely nothing to do with it. He is not the one who died on the cross, and he is obviously not the one who rose from the grave. So, the church involves two things: a death for atonement for sins, and a resurrection to give everlasting life to believers.

So, the Lord began to develop His disciples around this theme.

He taught them only what they could handle, because there was still a lot that He was going to teach and do with them namely:

1. He needed to die and rise from the dead,
2. He needed to send the Holy Spirit of God to lead the church.

At a lecture some day they asked Him, "where's the kingdom of God? He answered, "behold the kingdom of God is within you." (Luke

10:9) Someone jumped up and shouted: "you mean there's a government inside of me???" he asked Him in his confusion?

Funny! But he never laughed at him. When people came to him saying all kinds of things, He never made fun of them. He knew that the people were anxious and wanted wisdom and understanding. There were the educated, the uneducated, lawyers, doctors, business people, and those who simply never went to school, but no matter who you were He never said a word that will insult or make you feel uncomfortable. When you were with Him you felt welcome, you felt like this was the place to be, and you felt loved. You knew this was a Man who had all your answers of life. They were all His people, He created them, and He loved them all very dearly.

There was a day when Peter and Matthew met. The two hated each other. Matthew was the tax-collector, and the people of Israel hated tax-collectors with a passion. Peter was a tax-payer, and a businessman as a fisherman. They both knew that in the presence of Jesus it was a place for brotherhood. He was the Author of peace, and a lover of people, not a hater, so anyone who came to Him was a brother or sister.

He was a unifier not a divider. And He called them to Himself and did not say a word, and all they could say was simply, "Master!" in peaceful harmony. People found out where He was going to speak, and they took time off or vacations to go and hear Him. They skipped work just to attend the sessions. His sweet and soothing words were healing to weary souls. His words lifted them to new heights. So, they sat in for the ride. They listened to Him speak for days and days until He told them that they could go home. What a sweet presence. He was a magnet of the people. That's our God.

As He taught His disciples there was another group of spiritual beings, that was seemingly brought into the conversation. When He mentioned: "the gates of hades shall not prevail against it." (Matthew 16:18) After He made that statement, in my mind, He was referring directly to His angels, because He knew that persecutions would come after the church started. These persecutions were what He called the gates of hades. Angels knew all about the powers of darkness and they understood that He was speaking about these powers of darkness that would stir up trouble against His church.

THE DAY OF PENTECOST

The Lord had told the disciples that they should stay in the Upper Room until they received the Spirit of God from on High. He did not tell them when the Spirit would come, and how He looked like. That made for some suspense as they waited not knowing how He was to come. The Day of Pentecost was the day when there came a "Mighty Rushing Wind. (Acts 2:2) Since nobody knew how He looked like His arrival was a surprise to everyone. They thought it was a big storm, but they woke up with cloven tongues on their heads each speaking a strange language which the other person did not understand. The Mighty Rushing wind turned out to be the Mighty Holy Spirit, the ONE the Lord had described as the Comforter. When the Holy Spirit came He brought with Him the Church. It was the day when the young Church was born.

WHO IS THE HOLY SPIRIT?

The Holy is one of the Persons of Tri-um God. The designation of the Third Person of the Trinity is unbiblical, and incorrect. I believe He is simply one of the Persons of the Trinity, because Third Person implies ranking, which means of lower rank. That is not true, because Scripture teaches that they are equal in being. He is the Spirit of the Father and the Son, and He is the Power of God.

> The Bible also calls Him:
> The Promise of the Father;
> The Comforter;
> The Spirit of Truth;
> The Teacher of all things;
> The Reminder;
> The Spirit of Prophecy;
> The Spirit of Revelation'
> The Spirit of Wisdom;
> The Spirit of the Fear of the LORD;
> The Spirit of Power;

The Spirit of Love;
The Spirit of knowledge;
The Spirit of Intercession;
The Spirit of Life etc.

He also has the other attributes of the Father and the Son and He is the Head of the Church in the absence of Christ. Without Him there is no Church.

Having known who the Holy Spirit is, now let us define the Church in another way. It is group of believers in Christ who are filled with the Holy Spirit. Christ died for us, but the Spirit washes our sins with the water of regeneration, which completes the salvation process. Without the Holy Spirit no one can be saved, therefore there be no church. Scripture says, "Where two or more are gathered in My name I shall be in the midst. In His name, meaning the Father, the Son, and the Spirit.

BEING FILLED WITH THE SPIRIT

There are two ways of to be with the Holy Spirit:

1. Right after you have **truly believed** in Christ you are filled With the Holy Spirit, therefore you are born again. This is The most important requirement of salvation, and you are on your Way to heaven.
2. You need to be baptized with the Holy Spirit. This is the 2nd filling spoken of in (Acts 1:8; and Mark 16:17-18)

It is what the disciples had with tongues of fire on their heads on the Day of Pentecost. If you noticed, tongues of fire don't happen anymore, but the baptism of the Holy Spirit with the evidence of speaking in tongues. The baptism with the Holy Spirit is to give the Church power as specified in (Acts 1:8.) Many Pentecostal preachers have limited the gifts to just tongues, but it is not so. There are eight other gifts of the Holy Spirit apart from tongues. Speaking with other tongues is therefore, only one of the nine gifts of the Spirit.

The gift of tongues is an indication that the power of God is resident inside us. After this we must go out and minister believing that we have the gifts. You can believe for healing, miracles, etc. That is what I did, and many people have been healed in my ministry. With the presence of demonic powers all around us today the gifts are for healing, discernment of spirits, etc. They are the difference between a church and religion. They are the power of God that characterizes the Church.

As scripture says, the gifts are to give us power to witness to the world. I do not see Peter and other disciples dancing around because they spoke in tongues. They went right to work and started working miracles and winning converts to the faith. In summary, the gifts including tongues do four things:

a. Tongues glorify God;
b. Tongues win souls;
c. Tongues edify the Church;
d. Tongues are prayer weapon.

As soon as Peter and John were baptized, they didn't just stand there and speak with other tongues, they proceeded to heal people, work miracles, and to perform signs and wonders. Don't settle for speaking with tongues but go out and see what the Lord wants to do through you. The real wonder is when you use the power of God to cast out devils and do miracles. The Holy Spirit has given the gifts to the Church to solve all spiritual and physical problems in our societies, and there is nothing as powerful as the power of the Holy Spirit resident in the Church. The Church is not a religion it is a demonstration of the power of God. Every church should do what our Lord did, save souls, heal people do signs, wonders, and miracles.

WHAT IS THE CHURCH

Having spoken about the Holy Spirit let us return to the Church. The Church is a collection of **Spirit-filled** individuals, also known as the Body of Christ, wherever they may be. The church is not necessarily a building, as it is Spirit-filled individuals coming together. Therefore, the buildings you see on every street corner in America, and Europe are not necessarily Christian churches. Those are probably religious buildings, Judaic structures or Synagogues. The Lord did not build any Christian churches, nor did He leave instructions to erect buildings for the churches. He did not forget to leave instructions build one either. While He was still here on earth He preached in the temple, because people were there not because the temple was the church. God does not dwell in buildings built by human hands. The temple of the Holy Spirit is in every born-again Christian not in buildings.

When the Lord started Ministry, He sent the disciples out to preach door-to-door. (Matt. 10:5-17) He knew this was the only way the church would work. The reason our Lord did this was to stress the idea that the church was a soul-winning system. His intention was not for you and I to sit in comfortable buildings, called churches. No. In modern churches at least, eighty percent of the people have never won a soul. That is not what the Lord intended. The original apostles, except James, did not remain in Jerusalem. They went all over the world to proclaim the gospel. Here we are in the twenty-first century sitting in pews waiting for the Lord to come back. What do you think He is going to say to us?

The church is not necessarily a synagogue. That's Judaism. The church is not necessarily a building. I am not against buildings, but they have taken us completely out of what the Lord taught us. The Lord gave us a model, which is to go out and win souls, not sit around and relax as if we are in heaven already. I have spoken to people about evangelism until I am tired. Many of them will not dare to go out and talk to someone about Jesus. They are crippled by the devil with fear. You don't have to fear about the questions. The Lord is right there with you ask Him. Besides you don't to answer every question. Give them your phone number or take theirs. That way you create another conversation to get to know them better to minister to. You don't have to memorize the whole bible. If you don't know, just tell them you don' know.

I am a member of the Assemblies of God, but I was not saved the A/G. The Baptism with Holy Ghost is not as the born-again experience. Salvation brings the biggest change in any person's life: where an atheist becomes a strong man of God, a hardened murderer is converted to a sweet child of God, you know the rest. That is the most powerful thing the world has ever known. The Baptism with the Holy Spirit, however, brings a very different change. It gives us the power of God. That is the difference between a religious institution and the Church of Jesus Christ, and there is only one church. The church is not all about winning souls, but it is about the presence and the operation of the Holy Spirit. Consequently, a church must win souls, heal the sick, cast out devils, raise the dead, or come close to what our Lord did (see below).

The Baptism with the Holy Spirit brings another change. The Lord made a statement in His ministry that there's nobody the entire universe who can say that. When the woman with the issue of blood touch Him He asked who touched me? Peter and others said, "Lord, there are multitudes pushing and shelving you, and you say who touched me?" Then the Lord said, "Virtue has left me." You see, none of us can make that statement because virtue is not in any of us. He is the only One who has power.

The change that the Baptism brings is activated when you lay hands on the sick and they are healed. People see the sick person healed by your laying of hands, but you don't feel it, because the power is not in you. People say, wow this guy is something else, but you only something else, because the Holy Spirit gives you the anointing that causes people to be healed. To say the Baptism with the Holy Spirit has changed me is a lie, because you don't feel the change, but people see it because the Spirit of God causes the people to be healed, not you or me.

In my small ministry many people have been healed including my church through my laying of hands, but I have never felt anything. In my church one Sunday my pastor's wife came and asked me to go and pray with her for a crippled lady on a wheelchair. As we got there she prayed and as we were going to leave I told her, let me pray too. So, I laid my hands on the lady and prayed, and I told her, "you have told the church that you are healed, now get up and show them what the Lord has done." So, I took her by her hand and she got up. I walked her east and west of our sanctuary without the wheelchair for people to see. While we were walking people were shouting: "a miracle, a miracle, and a miracle." Now, I say that to say this, I have never felt virtue leave me at any time like the Lord felt. That is because none of us has that virtue, but people feel the anointing as the Holy Spirit activates it as you act by faith. The Spirit gives us these gifts, because they are not in us.

I want to see the true Pentecostal Church where all the gifts are in operation. There are many gatherings today including those for gays and lesbians, trans-gender folks, Mormons, Scientology, etc. Those are not churches. They are some types of social gatherings. In fact, most people all over the world don't understand what the word church means. I want to see the powerful Oral Robert Healing Tents, the power of God slaying saints in the Spirit in the Crusades of Catherine Coleman in the church again. Here is a little about the Lord's ministry to teach us what a church must do:

1. He won souls
2. He healed all who came to Him;
3. He cast out devils;
4. He calmed the storm;
5. He fed thousands with little or nothing;
6. He cleansed lepers;
7. He raised the dead, and many more miracles.

The church is not just about winning souls, as important as that is, it is about souls, miracles, signs and wonders, as He said, "greater things shall you do if I go to the father." (John 14:12) Our Lord set the example for us, Peter did it, Paul did it, as well as Philip, and so must we.

IMPORTANCE OF THE HOLY SPIRIT

The Lord knew that the Church of God could not be run by mere men. So, He sent His Holy Spirit, who is God. Christ did not come here to start another religion. There were already many of those. He wanted to start something that had divine power, so He called it His Church. I mentioned at the beginning of this chapter that there was no church without the Holy Spirit. His arrival started the Church of Jesus Christ. He is the church of Jesus Christ. These days are full of sinners gathered in buildings called churches. A building that houses gays, lesbians, transgender, and people who are not filled with Spirit of God is not a church. The institutions cannot do miracles, signs and wonders. Therefore, these are not churches. The church is to be run by the Spirit of God who has power. It means five things:

1. the church must depend on the Holy Spirit; Acts 2:4
2. participants must be filled with the Holy Spirit with the evidence of speaking in tongues; Acts 2:4
3. church leaders must be led by the Spirit; (John 16:13, 14:26)
4. ministry and spiritual gifts must be ministered by the Spirit;
5. leaders must be people who hear from the Spirit. John 14:26; 16:13.

We don't need intellectuals, but we need men and women who are full of the Spirit of the Living God.

Power is needed in the Church for wisdom, healing and other gifts given by the Holy Spirit. Our education and any other human systems cannot provide that spiritual power. The church is unique because of the Holy Spirit, nothing else. No other form of religion or human system has the Holy Spirit of God. Without Him there's nothing but religion. The church today is nothing but mostly a collection of religions.

THE ACTS AND POWER OF THE HOLY SPIRIT

Filled with Holy Spirit Peter addressed the crowds on the Day of Pentecost.

The people thought the apostles were nothing but a bunch of drunks, but the message was so powerful that it brought over three thousand converts, who put their faith in the Lord Jesus Christ that day alone. That was awesome. The new converts were also filled with the Holy Spirit. The question among the other apostles was, what is happening to Peter, and what had gotten into him? No one could believe their eyes, and ears at what was happening.

It was the power of the Holy Spirit. He became as bold as a lion the man their Master had seen. The Lord saw what no one else saw:

He saw a leader in Peter, no matter how many mistakes he made. Peter delivered a sermon that rocked the very foundation of the Church, and every apostle knew that a new thing had happened, something that was to change the world from that day forward.

THE POWER OF THE CHURCH – FIRST MIRACLE

When the Holy Spirit came, first the apostles spoke in the languages of the people who were watching Peter's sermon. You could see that something strange was in the air. Peter and John went to the Temple to pray the next morning, and there was a cripple there begging for alms at one of the gates. Peter said to him:

> "silver and gold, have I none but, such as I have, give I thee, in the Name of Jesus Christ of Nazareth rise up and walk." (Acts 3:6-7)

The man who had been begging at this gate for years suddenly jumped to his feet before a watching world. The lame man was healed of his paralysis, and he followed Peter and John into the Temple. The crowd went wild. No one had ever seen such a thing.

It was the first of its kind since the days of the Lord Himself. The News about the miracle went viral, as we say today. This man came asking for alms, but he left receiving his feet which he never had all his life. That was awesome. The man followed Peter and John into the Temple to the amazement of those thousands of onlookers. With this first miracle, the Holy Spirit had delivered on who He was.

THE FIRST PERSECUTION

You don't think the Spirit of God moved like that and Satan would go into hiding, do you? NOOOOOO! After the first miracle, the Sanhedrin, the Sadducees, the High priest, and the captain of the Temple did not take it lying down. They were very angry at the apostles for preaching and teaching the people using the name of Jesus concerning the Resurrection from the dead. They laid their hands on the apostles and put them in a prison holdup." In doing that they forbade them from preaching in that Name. Peter addressed the Sanhedrin, and he and the apostles vehemently vowed that they will not stop preaching in that Great Name. At the end of his address he said:

> "Nor is there salvation in any other, for there is no other Name under the heaven given among men by which we must be saved." (Acts 4:12)

There is no other Name, except the Name of Jesus.

SECOND PERSECUTION/ANGELIC INVOLVEMENT

A lot of things were happening to the young Church. It had just had its first miracle and thousands were being saved. Now came persecutions from the leadership of Israel. This is what the Lord meant when He said, "the gates of hades will not prevail against it." (Matthew 16:18) That was a classic, because you can't have the favor of the Lord, and expect Satan to take it lying down. He came at the church with ferocious persecutions. An argument began to take place among the opposition. Among them was a prominent man called GAMALIEL, Paul's professor, who told the other leaders:

> "we all have seen this before. Many false prophets had come and gone. If this is a true movement of God, then we cannot stop it, but if it a false movement it will die on its own." *(Acts 5:38-39)*

Wise words but he was wrong this time. This was a genuine move of God.

They kind of bought into this theory, and they could not leave the situation alone so, the persecutions continued, and eventually the high priest and the Sadducees grabbed the Christian leaders and put them in the common prison in Jerusalem, but the Church had no response. The next day they released them but forbade them from using that powerful name of Jesus.

That led to another address by Peter of the Sanhedrin and Jewish leaders. Consequently, the Church vowed to stand by the covenant which had been made since the time of Abrahamic. The Lord continued to add more converts to the Church and it grew very powerfully. But we are talking about Satan, a power much higher than the apostles. Their backs were against the wall. As the persecutions continue, the apostles were picked up and locked in the prison. They probably thought: "now, what are we going to do?" They did not know what the Lord was going to do with the situation.

Before they knew it, the angel of the Lord appeared. The appearance of the angel surprised the Church, but it also gave them the confidence they needed, knowing that God was with them during this time. There's no Religious Institution that is connected to God and His angels, except the Christian Church. It is unique. The angel came by night and the doors of the prison flung open as soon as the he appeared, and brought the apostles out saying: "go and stand and speak to the people at the temple the word of life." (Acts 5:20) They did as the angel told them. The high priest and the leaders got up to a big surprise: the prison was open, but everything else remained intact.

The apostles were gone. Where did they go? The city leaders later found them at the temple where they had been forbidden from preaching. The city leaders could not do anything, because of the people. They did not realize that they had more trouble than they could handle. They were up against Satan, the Israel leaders, temple guards, Pharisees, Sadducees, etc., but angelic power is far above physical and material earthly things, including human weapons, or any types of weaponry.

THE THIRD PERSECUTION

Now Herod had reached his hand to the extent that vexed the Church. He went as far as taking James and he killed him. When he saw that the Death of James pleased the temple leaders he sent and took Peter too. They put him between two prisoners bound with chains. "Behold, the angel of the LORD came upon Peter, and the light shown in the prison.

The angel said to Peter, "arise quickly, cast they garments about thee, and follow me."

Peter did as he was told, and the Angel took him to the Church where prayer was being made for him. (Acts 12:7-11)

Peter got to the Church unconscious. As the angel took him he was sleep-walking. When he arrived, a little girl told the disciples that Peter was at the door. The Church did not believe it, because they knew no one could take him out of the prison. The angel had released him, and it was real. After things cleared up there was no small joy and celebration for Peter's release.

Angelic involvement in the problems of the Church did not end with conquering persecutions, but it continued with making sure that the work of the Church grew to where it was needed, making sure, that leadership was in good hands of capable men like Peter, Paul, Philip to bring salvation to all people of Caesarea, and finally putting the last nail in the coffin of king Herod, the last enemy of the Church. On a set day king Herod was dressed up in his royal robes. He sat on his throne addressing a huge cheering crowd. As he spoke the people chanted say:

> "This is the voice of god, not the voice of a man!" As they chanted His head started swelling *with* pride. Immediately, the angel of the LORD struck Herod down, and the proud king suddenly dropped dead, and worms covered his whole body. The warms ate up his body. The crowd ran for their dear lives. This was done, because Herod failed to give glory to whom it was due, that is God. (Acts 12:21-23)

THE RISE OF PETER

It came to pass that the power of the Holy Spirit was so heavy on Peter. He was on fire, so to speak. The Lord did great wonders through the hands of the apostles in Jerusalem:

"so that they brought the sick into the streets and laid them on beds, and couches, that at least the shadow of Peter in passing by might fall on them. Also, a multitude gathered from the towns around Jerusalem, bringing the sick and those tormented by evil spirits, and all of them were healed."
(Acts 5:15-16)

When Peter's shadow hit them, they were completely healed. There was so much joy and celebration. It reminded me of what the Lord said earlier: "greater things shall you do as I go to the Father." Nobody ever saw anything like it. Scripture says the high priest and those with him were filled with indignation. They got up and laid their hands on the apostles and put them in the common Prison. That's when the angel of the Lord opened the prison and let them out and told them to go to the temple and speak the word of life.

PETER AND CORNELIUS

Peter became the leader that the Lord knew He would be. He was called everywhere, to pray, and preach the gospel of the Lord. He was sent to Caesarea by the angel to meet Cornelius. When he got there, he saw first-hand the Holy Spirit fall on the people while he yet spoke, and they spoke with other tongues. That startled him, and he learned for the first time, that God was no Respecter of persons. That encounter was the last angelic involvement in the affairs of the church. (Acts 10:4-46)

THE RISE OF PAUL – AFTER THE BAPTISM

During the struggle some of the apostles rose to prominence. We have seen Peter, and the next one was Paul. His coming to faith was like no other in Christian history. He was like the chief oppositionist of the Church because he was one of those who believed the apostles were just a bunch of radicals. He was breathing out threats, which slaughtered many of the disciples of the Lord. He went from house to house and brought Christian men and women to Jerusalem. On one of his trips on the Damascus Road He heard a call:

"SAUL, SAUL, SAUL, WHY DO YOU PERSECUTE ME." (Acts 9:4)

Before he knew it, he was knocked down, and blinded by the power of God. As mentioned earlier, he had thought of the disciples as violent people who persecuted his Jewish faith. He now found out that he was persecuting God's people. He who was labeled the "chief killer of Christians" became one of them. He was right then converted, and commissioned to the gentiles by the Lord commissioned to the gentiles by the Lord, but it was hard for the Church to trust him, because of the havoc he had caused.

Later, the Holy Spirit was all over him, and he is credited with writing almost the whole of the New Testament Church. Scripture teaches that the Lord did special miracles through the hands of Paul. He raised the dead and picked up snakes with his hands etc. At the pinnacle of his ministry people brought handkerchiefs and aprons and took them home to the sick and they were healed. Unclean spirits knew his name. There were other prominent leaders that rose up in the Church at that time, such as Barnabas, etc.

THE RISE OF PHILIP – AFTER BAPTISM

The angel of the Lord spoke to Philip saying: "arise and go toward the south on the way that goes down from Jerusalem, to Gaza which is desert." (Acts 8:26) There's an ETHIOPIAN, a man who was a man of authority. Philip went and ministered to the man, who later became saved and received the Holy Spirit. The Holy Spirit later caught up Philip from Jerusalem to Caesarea in Rome, and he preached to the Romans there, and the gospel went viral for the first time. Philip disappeared in that event. The angel of the Lord in sending Philip to Samaria, and Caesarea triggered the first international mission.

LAST ANGELIC INVOLVEMENT

Angelic involvement with the early church ended right after the angels of God took out Herod, the enemy of the Church. We discussed Herod earlier. Angelic involvement came at a time when the Church was having a tough time. Everything the apostles did was met with resistance from city leaders, the Sadducees, and the high priest. At first it seemed as if the opposition was succeeding, but with the arrival of angels the rules of game were changed, so to speak. It gave the apostles the help they needed, and it also gave them the confidence knowing that as Christians they were connected to our Lord and His angels. Not only was the Church established in Israel, but they made sure it went world- wide.

CHAPTER 11

Lessons From Angels

LESSONS LEARNED

Throughout this book we can truly say that we have learned a number of lessons about angels including: what they are and what they do. The first thing we learned was that angels are spirit beings, meaning they have no flesh and blood. They were created to live in heaven with God. That tells me that they are a higher order creature than we are in wisdom, and power. There's no comparison.

The next thing that we learned was that God created angels to be His messengers, to serve Him in any way He wants. What do I mean by serving Him in any way He pleases? That means they can do anything, and they can do it with excellence. The difference is they can do everything we do here on earth, but that much better than we can ever do. They are messengers, warriors, and builders, etc.

LIVING IN HIS PRESENCE

Angels live in the presence of God. What does that mean? First of all, the presence of God is in heaven and that means everything including: love, joy, and peace, etc. Living there you get to enjoy life to the fullest. I believe I can say something about that joy and peace from my own experience in a dream I had a few years ago.

I had a dream once and in that dream the Lord came. It was the Second Coming of Christ. The Lord was just floating in the air. His feet did not touch the floor. The band was playing, and there were all kinds of angels there. I call them angels, because there was nobody human. I mean you see people, but you don't know where they were coming from. There were hundreds of thousands or perhaps millions. Then we started to dance. We danced, and we danced for days, and days. We did not get tired, we did not get hungry, and we were not thirsty. The joy was like living water, oozing out of our stomachs. I call it joy uncontainable. We were overwhelmed by it. I think the Lord showed me a little bit of heaven. When I woke up the next morning I was very angry, because I did not want to wake up. I will never forget that dream.

That is what angels enjoy in heaven. What I told you is just a very little part of it. There's much more of that in the bible, and nobody in this side of heaven can give you the full story. Those who say angels want to dwell with the sons of men are mistaken. Those were evil angels. I don't believe anyone who has tasted heaven would want to live on earth with all our problems. Thank God he saved us, so we can go and live with Him forever and ever in His wonderful and glorious presence.

LESSON IN LOVE

We learned that angels inhabit the throne of God where there is among other things abundant of love. When Christ came it was God's extension of His love to mankind. He gave us more than love. He gave us the very life that we did not have. We were dead in our sins, but He came to atone for those sins. In doing that He also took away all our bondages of addictions of drugs, and alcohol, etc. He came to teach us how to live in peace with one another. All we knew was to kill each other, and to live the life that the evil one taught us.

His mission to save mankind changed us completely as His love was imputed into our hearts and transformed us into children of God. Another thing that was imputed into us was His righteousness, turning us into the children of light. He loved us so much that though we repaid

Him with death but He rose from the dead to take away the power of death, and to give us everlasting life. The angels could not die for us, so they gave us someone who could. The lesson of the cross was a valuable lesson that we needed.

LESSON OF A CHILD

One lesson we learned was the humility of angels. Their attitude is like children in terms of trusting God. Children have complete faith, and fully trusting. They are like Isaac, Abraham's son who allowed himself, to be the sacrifice, a type of the Lamb of God. That day Isaac asked his father: "the fire and the wood are here, where is the lamb?" Abram answered: "God himself will provide the lamb." (Gen.22:7-8) It was up to Abram to thrust the knife, but as far as the sacrifice was concerned Isaac was ready, but before he do it an angel was there showed him a ram in the thicket. Abraham trusted God to send the lamb, and Isaac trusted His father that he would not kill him.

Angels are the same way. Whatever God wants them to do is automatically done, no ifs, or buts. They know that God cannot mislead them. They trust Him completely. We need to have that kind of trust in God. If we did, we would never have any problems. That's why God trusts His angels too.

Like children angels do not have material possessions, because they do not need them, and sometimes these things give us a false sense of power. They have nothing, and they control nothing, that way, they are not bound by anything. That is because they have learned their lessons well. There's freedom in living a life that is not dependent. So, they cannot be tempted, because they want nothing. Satan tempts us because he knows we desire material things.

Due to their trust for their Master, they are very obedient. We need to trust God, and to obey Him completely too. They go wherever they are sent saying: "I have been sent." They are never too old, or too big to obey instructions. They love everybody, and everybody is important to them. They have no inferiority or superiority complexes. Everybody is completely humble. They serve their Master in whatever He pleases. This is what they are made for.

If one angel gets promoted, they simply understand that God loves everybody. So, they rejoice for the one that has been promoted. To get envious is sin. That's why they are holy. We have shown you that there are hierarchies of angels, but if one is promoted they rejoice with the one, because there is no real difference. No matter how high any angel gets, everything comes down to angel being a messenger. They are content with being with that.

Children understand that they know nothing, and so they seek knowledge, and understanding from the elders. God trusts His angels and He lives among them, just as Christ lived with His disciples. He allows them to ask questions with a pure heart, with the sole aim of gaining knowledge. They are like sponges soaking on every bit of knowledge from God they might gain. Wherever they are sent they go without questioning, and whatever they are sent to do, they do it without questioning.

They are like children who never grow up. It is like they intentionally refuse to grow up, because they are so humble. They have no opinions of their own, because the Master is always right, because He is omniscient and they are not. They do whatever the Master has sent them to do whether it makes sense of not, because ultimately the Master is always right.

Their honor and respects for the Master encourages them to give Him their lives. He is the Good Master, who gives His life for His servants, in the same way they are the good servants who give their life to the master. It is a two-way situation. If you ever meet the LORD, you would think that they live together as friends. You couldn't tell who the Master is when they are together unless a question arises as to who is the master. When Mary Magdalene saw them on Resurrection Day she could not tell who the master was. Their love for Him compels them to do whatever pleases Him.

LESSONS IN HUMILITY

We human beings must learn the all-important lesson of humility. The way to do that is to become children as He said: "except you be converted and become as little children you shall not enter the kingdom of heaven." (Matthew 18:3) That is because in His presence there's no room for pride. He goes back to the lesson of a child. Children are like sponges. They soak on whatever they are given without any arguments. That is because they know and trust what they are told. A little child knows that he or she has nothing, in terms of money or other resources, so they humbly accept whatever they are given. If you give them nothing that is good too. What makes them happy is so small. Most of the time all they really want from their parents is the truth. Angels already have that truth in God.

They take in whatever is offered. No arguments and no preferences. They are easy to teach and easy to mold. They are God's favorite students. Whatever is given is great. Christ Himself was a Model of Humility, and His angels are the same way. Humility is probably the first topic on their training manual.

MESSENGER/SERVANT

One lesson we might all learn is being a servant. Angels are forever servants. As we saw a servant is someone who has given of himself or herself to serve his or her Master. That is similar to a humble person or someone who has voluntarily emptied himself or herself of their reputation. There's an emptying here.

The great thing about angels is that they have very little or nothing and they are not looking to possess anything. Some of us have lots of money, possession, education, and all kinds of things. That sometimes creates a reputation. What happens is these things bring pride. The angels we see do not even wear shoes. Sometimes even something like that can stand in our way of being humble. You see we think humility is all about serving other people. That is true, but it goes further than that. You could serve people and still be prideful.

Scripture says our Lord emptied Himself of His reputation when He became a man. He is our model of a servant. Angels are like humble, and simple. They have simple lives and are satisfied with being that way. They are easy to please. There is something about angels that is inviting, and that makes them approachable. A servant of God must demonstrate these qualities.

GOD'S HELPING HANDS

One of the greatest things about God is the help He gives us, and angels are His helping hands. All we can do is ask for it and He will do it. Angels are like signed up for the LORD's charity. Wherever there's a need that is their work and that's what they were created for. The rich or poor qualify. When it comes down to it all ranks of angels are messengers as messengers they are miracle workers, healers, prayer warriors, or angelic warrior their mission is to spread God's love around the universe. They may or may not know us personally, but no matter what our needs are their hands are open to whoever needs the services. They hold no grudges, nor keep a list of wrong doings. Their help is available to anyone.

MINISTERING SPIRITS

Angels do whatever it takes to please their master. Their job is to serve us as God directs. They are self-less at this. It may mean coming to earth to solve human problems like rescuing a person trapped in a deep valley, or one who is drawing in a deep ocean they do it. Things happen that could cause us harm, they are there to prevent us from being harmed. I mean whatever His pleasure is they are always up to the challenge. They travel faster than the speed of light, and they do things so fast that we don't even notice. They have given themselves to God, so they are available to be used for His pleasure.

I believe that the pool of angels is so vast in heaven, so everyone is dying to serve. If selected, it is considered as an opportunity to perform an assignment. As I said before, service is their duty and their reward. It gives them the opportunity to come before the master, and to show Him what you have. We humans want to serve God for money and other things, but God has angels in heaven dying to do His work.

Ministering is probably what guardian angels and other angels do. They are specifically created to provide any help for the redeemed. It's not a big thing for His angels to serve Him. They do anything to serve. We must know that all people were created to serve God, and we could learn something the selflessness of angels.

WORSHIPPING WITH FERVENCY

One lesson we can all learn from angels is worship. They give themselves to worship. As spirits this is ideal for God, as He seeks those who worship in spirit and truth. They are the model for worship. Scripture says, they worship twenty-four hours per day, seven days a week, twelve months per year, and forever and ever. Their whole life is consumed with worship, and there's not a moment at the throne of God when worship is not going on.

Thank God He created them to worship the way they do. That says a lot about their energy levels. We humans do not have the DNA of angels, but He created all beings to worship Him. His pleasure is their joy, and life. Angelic life is a daily sacrifice in the service of the LORD. No wonder it says, worship must be holy, and acceptable to Him. We could learn like the angels do to be a sacrifice in a way that is acceptable to God.

That means not a minute goes by in the throne of God without worship. We humans do not have the energy that angels have. I don't think God expects humans to worship Him the way angels do, yet this is a lesson we can learn, because we stand to gain much from worship. Angels are never sick, so their worship is their duty.

They are right there with God, so they already enjoy the presence of God. Worship completes us, because when the Spirit of God moves humans are healed from sickness and delivered from addictions. We don't need the dry worship services that we are seeing in churches today.

That is because of our inability to worship as we should. Yes, we are not angels, but we need to worship to a certain level, so that God can give us the benefits that come with worship.

So, what do we do when one of the expectations of our Maker is to worship Him? In the days of king David worship services were a real treat for the people. Service went on for several days, and the glory of the Lord showed up. As the people basked in the glorious presence of the Lord they experienced joy, and miracles. We must increase our worship, so the Spirit can move among us.

In Acts Chapter 20 Paul went to a worship service in Troas in the New Testament on a Sunday morning. The Service went through all the night of the first day through the next day. One guy fell from the third floor to the first and died. Paul prayed over the guy and raised him from the dead. The guy's name was EUTYCHUS. That is proof that the presence of the Lord brings rewards. We are needy people, and the presence of God meets our needs. I believe that extended worship periods bring a heavy movement of the Spirit of God. That is really the reason that we worship. I think churches must follow Acts 20 model.

Without worship we can never experience the move of God, and we will continue to be as dry in our services, and we could never have the benefits that come with the movement of the Holy Spirit. There's no need going to a church service where there is no movement of the Holy Spirit which comes with worship. Our Pastors must know that we can no longer afford empty dry services. They must be trained to discern the presence and movement of God and prolong services accordingly. I know that I need to worship for at least five hours on Sundays. We must be hungry for a move of God. I know angels are always hungry to worship their God. That is a lesson for all of us.

CHAPTER 12

God and Angels

ANGELIC WITNESS is partly about the Incarnation of the Lord Jesus Christ, and about angels. The first two chapters speak about the King of Glory, Jesus Christ, who left heaven and came to earth for the sole purpose of dying on a cruel cross to save mankind from of sins committed against God. His first advent shocked His own people, the people of Israel, who have believed in God since the dawn of history but had never seen Him in person. As a result, He was rejected after living on earth for thirty-three and a half years, all because He took human form.

The book picked out seven titles of deity which were given before the child was born. It compares the titles with the attributes of God, and declares that Christ is the same God of the universe that they have known, but they still rejected Him, putting Him to death by the same people He came to save. The Book bears witness of His birth, earthly life, activities, teachings, and miracles He performed among the people.

The angels walked with Him during His entire ministry and attested to the teachings He gave to His followers. In the end they watched Him die and buried, and they were the first on the scene to witness His glorious Resurrection. He lived on earth for a brief period, and then ascended into heaven.

While the disciples were gazing into the sky the angel of the Lord appeared to them saying: **"Men of Galilee, why do you stand gazing**

into the sky? This same Jesus who has been taken from you into heaven will come back again as you have seen Him go into heaven."

Angelic Witness tells the biblical story of the creation of angels by the Lord Jesus Christ: who angles are, and what they do. It discusses angelic types, hierarchies, being, power and work. The book also speaks of their incredible service to mankind through God. A must-read part of the book is the fall of satan and other evil angels.

After the ascension the angels came to help establish the New Church. Angelic involvement ensured the success of the establishment, and that continued until it spread to the whole world. The book ends when the last enemy of Jesus Christ was put to death, and it continued in the hands of capable leaders such as Peter, Philip, and Paul, etc.

SCRITURAL GLOSSARY

OLD TESTAMENT

Genesis	3:14-15
Exodus	19:6
Numbers	12:6
Daniel	9:20-24; 10:6,13
2 Kings	19:35
1 Chronicles	11:12-44
1 Chronicles	21:15-16
Psalm	103:20-21
Psalm	110:4
Psalm	104:4
Proverb	2:6
Ezekiel	1:1-26; 10:5
Ezekiel	28:13-19
Isaiah	6:1-6; 11:2
Jeremiah	33:3;
2 Samuel	14:20

NEW TESTAMENT

Gospel of Matthew	4.11
Matthew	28:2-6; 28:31 28:7, 24:31;
	13:30, 13:41; 13:49; 16:13-18.
Mark	16:5-6 8:38
Luke	1:30-56; 2:9-14; 16:1-13;
Luke	24:4-5; 6-7
John	4:14-24; 5:4; 20:12-14; 21:12-45;
	John 18:36
1 Corinth	12:7-30
II Corinth	10:4-5
2 Peter	2:4
Acts.	2:11
Acts	*5:4, 5:19-20, 5:15*
Acts	8:26
Acts	10:3; 10:22, 10:44
Acts	11:15
Acts 12:7-10; 12:23	
Ephesians	2:14
Philippians	4:7
Hebrews	1:7; 1:14
Hebrews	5:6
1 Thessalonians	4:16
Revelation	4:6-9; 5:2
Revelation	7:1-4
Revelation	8:2; 9:11; 10:1-3
Revelation	12:7-9
Revelation	20:1-2

BIOGRAPHICAL NOTES

RALPH T. EBOTMANYINAW has preached to small audiences starting from door-to-door in Miami Florida, after his salvation to the office where he worked at Cuyahoga Job and Family Services, he operated a bible class on the job. Other audiences include churches, and in Nursing Homes in the City of Cleveland, and Parma Ohio. Only the heavens know how many were saved. Joined by his Brother Paul Mosher, we opened a bible class at Work, taught, and supervised a Breakfast for the homeless, at Calvary Reformed Church. Paul has been a great friend and brother for many years. He is currently the Center Manager at Cuyahoga County Job and Family Services. It's hard to find a friend so faithful, Paul has served with me for over twenty. We are not theologians, or even very qualified people in ministry, but Paul and I have a heart for the glorious gospel of our Lord. Ralph taught Sunday-School for over six years at Calvary and Paul and I were called to the Nursing Home Ministry in 2005. During these years we have preached, and witnessed, and the Lord confirmed His work with salvations and healings. He shares his life with his beautiful daughter, RACHEL EBOTMANYINAW, who is the love of his life.

I have always had a fascination with angels. I have not seen angels in person, but I have seen them in my dreams. I know you are thinking, this is spooky now that he is speaking about dreams. I know that many people dismiss dreams in western civilization, but don't forget there's a lot about dreams in the holy bible, not because God is spooky, but because dreams are spiritual. The kind of dreams that I am talking about are those that God gives me. I believe that everybody dreams, because every human being is spirit by nature.

ANGELIC WITNESS is the second of two books, but Ralph is not really a writer. He is one whose desire is to preach the gospel of the Lord and His Love across this world. If the Lord tarries, I will continue to write until He comes. It is my greatest pleasure to proclaim the gospel of the Lord Jesus Christ and Print His Name across this world.

ABOUT THE AUTHOR

Ralph T. EBOTMANYINAW was born from Cameroon, in West Africa. Ralph moved to the USA to pursue college studies at Western Oregon University. After graduation I moved to Idaho State University with graduate plans, but these plans were interrupted by the I.N.S. for being out of status. He moved to Miami Florida where he fell into the loving arms of the Lord Jesus Christ and he gave his heart to the Lord and became a born-again in 1992. The Born-again experience was the greatest that ever happened in my life. After that I started Street Ministry where I began to minister to friends in the city. I moved to Cleveland, Ohio, on April 20th, 1994. In Cleveland Ralph continued with ministry at work to friends on the job and clients on the job which got me in trouble with supervisors where I worked as an eligibility and alien specialist with the Cuyahoga Job and Family Services.

At work I was joined by my good friend and Brother Paul Mosher to form a Bible study Class on the job. Ralph was called by the Lord to Calvary Reformed Church where among other things, taught Sunday-School and together with Paul we organized a Breakfast for the Homeless for several years. At Calvary Ralph was ordained elder, co-chaired the Worship Committee, and was an active member of the Consistory and the choir.

While at Western I met Judge and Mrs. Robert Gardner who treated me as a member of their family at a time when I had no family. They paid for projects in their church, and they worked to see the completion of the work. I remember when we painted and roofed their church building. They were very active members in the committees of the church. You see it takes a tremendous amount of love to serve God. Rob and Mrs. Gardner had that love. That stuck with me. After I got saved

I began to do the same thing. I saw in them the best of America. Rob is in heaven now, and I know we will see him again soon.

Paul and I were called by the Lord to preach in three Nursing Homes in the cities of Cleveland and Parma, Ohio. We have been witnesses to the amazing work of the Lord in healings and salvations for several years. Ralph is currently an author, and his first work was the POWER OF FAITH, and the second book titled ANGELIC WITNESS will be published in 2022. His Writings are a continuation of his teaching on a broad number of subjects. The main reason for writing is to testify of the great work of his Mighty Lord, and Savior Jesus Christ who died and gave His life for all mankind. BLESSED BE HIS HOLY NAME.

WORKS CONSULTED

Angels in Judaism: Wikipedia.

Dr. Jack Graham   ANGELS: WHO THEY ARE, AND IMPORTANCE

Benny HYNN   Good Morning Holy Spirit

W.E. Vines: Expository Dictionary of New Testament Words;

Dr. William Smith: Smith's Bible Dictionary;

Kenneth Barker, Donald Burdick, John STEK, Ronald Youngblood: THE NIV STUDY BIBLE.

Dr. SCOFIELD:

    THE ORIGINAL KING

    JAMES VERSION

    Of the BIBLE

Printed in the United States
by Baker & Taylor Publisher Services